Creative ~~Writing~~ *Cooking*

Recipes from the Authors You Love

Edited by Nancy Gotter Gates

Compiled by the Writers' Group of the Triad
Ralph Myers, President

Illustrated by Tim Rickard

Cookbook Committee: Nancy Gates, Judy Clement, Dorothy Eggert, Judi Hill, Karen McCullough, Ralph Myers, Carol Rawleigh, Peggy Rooks

Down Home Press, Asheboro, North Carolina

Copyright 1994 by Nancy Gotter Gates
First Printing, September 1994

All rights reserved. No part of this book may be reproduced by any means without permission of the publisher, except for brief passages in reviews and articles.

ISBN 1-878086-32-4

Library of Congress Catalog Card Number 94-068684
Printed in the United States of America

Book design: Mason R. Harris
Cover design: Tim Rickard

Baked Camel recipe exerpted from *Water Music* by T. Coraghessen Boyle, Copyright 1982 by T. Coraghessen Boyle. Used by permission of Little, Brown and Company.

Zucchini-feta Pancakes recipe exerpted from the *Moosewood Cookbook* by Mollie Katzen, Copyright 1992 by Mollie Katzen. Used by permission of Ten Speed Press, Berkeley, CA 94707.

Twemy-seven igredient Chili recipe exerpted from the *27-Ingredient Chili Mystery* by Nancy Pickard, Copyright by Nancy Pickard. Used by permission of Delacorte Press.

Byzantine Artichokes recipe exerpted from *Cold Cuisine*, Copyright 1981, 1990 by Helen Hecht. First published by the Ecco Press in 1990. Reprinted by persmission.

Down Home Press
P.O. Box 4126
Asheboro, N.C. 27204

Foreword

Food! The images pervade our written word from the forbidden *Pommes au Couteau* of Genesis down to Nancy Pickard's *The 27 Ingredient Chili Con Carne Murders*.

Lucullan delights spread across the table of our inner eye when we read of Mrs. Cratchit's Christmas pudding; the menu of "apricocks and dewberries, purple grapes, green figs, mulberries and honey-bags" from which Titania orders dinner for Bottom; Millay's *Thanksgiving Dinner* of steaming winter roots; or Proust's well-remembered *madeleines* soaked in a "decoction of lime flowers."

And when we write, we do not let our characters go hungry for long because food offers yet another insight into personality and values: do they eat potato chips and candy bars on the run, or do they linger over the gold-tasseled a la carte menu of a four-star restaurant? Are they red-meat-and-potatoes, or brown-rice vegans? Are they knowledgeable about vintages and labels, or will they drink anything as long as it's sweet and carbonated? Do they cook from scratch when they eat in, or do they send out for Chinese?

Gathered between the covers of this book are dozens of recipes. Some are whimsical, some dead serious, but all are as idiosyncratic as the writers who agreed to share them.

Sample their dishes.

Sample their writing.

May they whet your appetite for more!

–Margaret Maron

Gail Galloway Adams

Gail Galloway Adams won the 1988 Flannery O'Connor Award for her collection of short stories The Purchase of Order. *Named Outstanding Teacher of 1993 at the College of Arts and Sciences at West Virginia University, she is currently at work on a novel.*

[From a work-in-progress.]

Three daughters were in their mother's kitchen making gumbo. Okra was heaped in a woody pile in the middle of the large chopping block; already a large bowl of it had been sliced into rounds and the big chef's knife was scummy with okra sap.

"Do you remember that man who used to grow okra with Granny?"

"That old bent-over-like-an-ironing board man?"

Yes, Mr. Walls, no, not Walls, it was Walker. Was not. It was something else like Joseph Conrad. No, it was Marley, the Mother called from the other room. Mr. Marley like the Ghost of Christmas past. The horror the horror one sister muttered. Yes poor old crippled man. Do you remember, the Mother said coming into the room and stopping to survey the flecks of green red and brighter green and white. I don't like so many people coming in and taking over my kitchen. People! People she calls us. We're your daughters. Well yes but...Did you do the peppers? she asks peering in the bowl of scallions suspiciously. Yes, the oldest daughter answers, they are in the icebox now and yes tomatoes are in there too and the garlic and the celery and anything else you can think to ask about and what were you about to say about Mr. Marley that bent over old man? He looked just like a little old crow didn't you think, asked one sister. No, I always thought when I was near him that if I wanted I could rest my arm on his back just like I did with that wolf hybrid I told you about, the one with the sly yellow eyes that looked at everybody like prey. The knife slams down with a thud. What is the story? one daughter asks. Well, the Mother says, remember the time I drove up to get Granny and bring her home from Graham and early too? It was because she was worried about Mr. Marley. He couldn't do for himself. Do you remember she said "He'll never be able to pick that okra all by himself and if it stays too long it'll get big and woody and then no one could eat it not even your little pig, and she didn't even remember that Petunia was dead? Is that the story about Mr. Marley? one daughter asked. It seemed lame to her.

No, that's not the story the middle sister said. Mine is entirely different. I always thought he looked like one of those old fashioned photographers the way the ends of his bolo tie hung down like two legs of a tripod: throw a cape over him and you'd expect to have a bright flash in your eye. No, what about the elephant man? the mean sister said and the knife whacked whacked against the okra pods lined up one two three four. Little hard green hats at the ends bounced to the floor. That's the exact color of Granny's car that she insisted I drive up to Graham in; the same color as Spanish olives, they're too salty for me, the mother shuddered.

Shrimp and Okra Bisque

1/4 cup plus 2 Tbsp. vegetable oil, in all
3/4 lb. okra, sliced 1/4 inch thick (3 cups sliced in all; use frozen if fresh not available)
3/4 cup finely chopped onions
3/4 cup finely chopped green bell peppers
1/2 cup finely chopped celery
4 Tbsp. unsalted butter
2 tsp. minced garlic
1/4 cup all purpose flour
5-1/2 cups, in all, canned chicken broth

1/2 cup finely chopped green onions
3 doz. peeled medium shrimp, about 3/4 lb.

Seasoning mix:
    3 whole bay leaves
    2 tsp. salt
    1-1/2 tsp. dry mustard
    1-1/4 tsp. white pepper
    1 tsp. ground red pepper (cayenne)
    1 tsp. dried thyme leaves
    1/2 tsp. black pepper
    1/2 tsp. dried sweet basil leaves

Combine the seasoning mix ingredients in a small bowl and set aside. In a 4-quart saucepan, heat 1/4 cup of oil over high heat for 1 minute. Stir in 2 cups of the okra; cook until browned, about 5 minutes, stirring occasionally. Stir in the onions, bell peppers and celery and cook 1 minute. Add the butter and cook 1 minute; then stir in the garlic and cook 1 minute more. Now add the seasoning mix and stir well; continue cooking over high heat for 3 minutes, stirring frequently and scraping pan bottom well. Add the remaining 2 Tbsp. oil and the flour; stir and scrape the pan bottom well. Continue cooking until well browned, stirring frequently, about 2 minutes. Stir in 1-1/2 cups of the broth and scrape the pan bottom well; then add rest of the broth (4 cups) and stir well. Bring to a boil, stirring often. Boil 2 minutes, then lower heat and simmer 5 minutes, stirring occasionally. Stir in the remaining 1 cup okra. Continue simmering 10 minutes, stirring occasionally. Add the green onions and simmer 3 minutes. Remove from heat. Add the shrimp, turn heat to medium, and simmer just until shrimp turn pink, about 1 minute. Serve immediately, allowing about 3/4 cup for each serving. Or ladle over rice as main course. Or if not flush you can leave out the shrimp and just have okra gumbo. Serves 8. This is an easy dish once you have the usual Cajun triumverate of vegetables chopped.

Ranee

[From a writing exercise.]

"One should not ever take the insects for granted as they too suffer and toil." She remembered exactly how the old man's voice had sounded and all other memories that she thought she'd put away: nights when prayers and chanting seemed endless, when the stench of incense was so thick she woke from a trance to wonder would she ever take a breath again? Sometimes in those days when she'd lived under the sway of another came flashes of clarity and she'd be struck by the idea that this was her life now, she was living it. If it happened during field work she'd pause and look at her hands, broken nails, calloused skin. What am I doing holding a hoe? What am I doing farming? She'd steal a moment to look at the sky, no longer than that because you were docked if you stopped working long enough for Bagwan to see. It was always that "off-we-go-into-the-wild-blue-yonder" sky; that's what her first father had called it. And she'd think where is the person who was me before this?

Once when she'd had the hated children duty which was so hard—nothing ever to do, never anything to teach them, only the panjans could teach—she'd moved the group outdoors into the back courtyard. There she'd trimmed sticks and showed them how to write though she knew it was forbidden. One little boy, she remembered his name—Ganesh—poked his stick into a hole in the dry and dusty soil. He held it steady and watched ants swarm up and over to cover his small chapped hand.

"Stop, you'll get stung," she shouted and snatched the stick away. He stared solemnly and repeated what they all were taught, chanted over and over: "They so small and we so large. Let them harm us for awhile." His child's eyes were the wild blue of the sky and blank with that learning and she turned from him thinking what have I done to my life?

O Calcutta Cheese Spread

1 8-oz. package of cream cheese
1 cup of grated sharp cheddar cheese
1/2 tsp. garlic powder
1 tsp. to 1 Tbsp. curry powder (start with lesser amount and add to your personal taste)
1-2 Tbsp. sherry (can add more or less to taste but don't make it too runny)
1 bottle Major Grey's Chutney
chopped scallions as garnish

Mix all the above ingredients well, adding more curry powder or sherry to your taste. Once the cheeses are blended the spread will be a light golden color. Put it on a serving plate and shape it into a circle about one inch high. Now spread Major Grey's Chutney across the top, covering to the edge; be sure and get pieces of mango on the top. Sprinkle with scallions and make it look pretty. Surround with cracked pepper crackers or flatbreads. Have a knife available for spreading it thin. It's an unusual and wonderful combination of flavors that can be made with low calorie/no fat cream cheese and cheddar cheese and will taste just as delicious.

Jean Auel

A technical writer with no background in paleontology, Jean Auel quit her job at 40 to write a "short story" about prehistoric cave dwellers. That story turned into her first novel, Clan of the Cave Bears, *which was followed by three more highly successful novels on the same theme.*

On Potatoes

It was often thought that prehistoric people—hunters/gatherers—lived a meager existence, "grubbing for roots," etc. I've tried to show in my books that the way people lived before agriculture was not necessarily less, in any way, only different. And we still "grub for roots"—onions, carrots, potatoes....

One of my favorite ways to cook potatoes is to peel and boil, in separate pots, some potatoes and some carrots. Saute chopped onions in butter until soft, then mash them all together, or mash separately and mix together, adding a little milk, salt, and pepper to taste. Proportions and quantities are not all that important, but if you use more carrots than potatoes, it is a different dish from the one that uses more potatoes than carrots. I favor more potatoes.

Speaking of potatoes, when I was a kid growing up in Chicago, in the summer the neighborhood children, boys and girls, often made bonfires on empty lots. I don't recall adult supervision, but it may have been there. Each of us would go home and come back with a potato, which was put into the bottom of the fire just in its skin (this was before the days of "tin foil"). If done right, it would come out black on the outside, and cooked in the middle, and was eaten just like that, with no salt, pepper, butter, or anything else. We thought they were delicious! I think it used to make us feel that we were somehow more grown-up and independent to know we could cook something ourselves, and perhaps that we were living a little closer to nature, doing something that smacked of "survival."

And while I'm at it, the best french fries I have ever eaten were made from scratch, with raw potatoes, while we waited and watched in a small restaurant in the foothills of the Pyrenees in France.

Ellyn Bache

Ellyn Bache's short stories, articles and reviews have appeared in McCall's, Ascent, Southern Humanities Review, *and various other magazines and newspapers. Her first novel,* Safe Passage, *has been made into a movie starring Susan Sarandon and Sam Sheppard scheduled for release late in 1994. She is founder of North Carolina Fiction Syndicate.*

I have a reputation as a really terrible cook. I have raised four children, and whenever they go off to college they always comment on how wonderful the food is in the dining hall—which gives you some idea. All the same, I do cook every night so these are recipes that absolutely work every time.

I hate cakes made from mixes. I think they taste like perfume, and I don't think they're any easier to make than cakes from scratch. Mary Lou's Chocolate Cake is one I make whenever I need a cake, and it always comes out tasting delicious. If you frost this with some kind of chocolate icing, it's a true chocoholic's delight, but in our house, it usually gets eaten before it gets iced at all. (Mary Lou, by the way, was not a character in my fiction, but a friend of my mother-in-law, a farm wife in Indiana who cooked magnificent meals for the farm hands every day.)

Curried Butternut Squash Soup is something I make for myself and for my sophisticated women friends. My husband and kids won't touch it. It's the sort of nutritious dish Alona, in my novel, *Festival in Fire Season*, would have fixed for her ailing grandmother. It's also rich and tasty without being very caloric.

Vegetable Casserole is another dish I make mainly for myself, although my brother-in-law also likes it, bless his heart. You can use different vegetables in this, whatever you have on hand. I've used carrots, which are nice (layer them toward the bottom), and once I made it without green peppers, but I do think it's better with the peppers. (Also, the potatoes, onion, and garlic give it its distinctive texture and taste.)

Mary Lou's Chocolate Cake

1 cup hot water
2 squares unsweetened chocolate
2 cups sugar
2 cups flour
1 tsp. baking soda
1 1/2 tsp. baking powder
1 tsp. salt
1/2 cup vegetable oil
2 eggs
1/2 cup buttermilk
1 tsp. vanilla extract

Preheat oven to 350 degrees. Put chocolate in small bowl and pour hot water over. Set aside. In large bowl, combine flour, sugar, baking soda, baking powder, and salt. Pour chocolate mixture over it and mix till blended. Add oil, eggs, buttermilk and vanilla. Mix till blended. Pour into one 13"x9" pan. Bake 35-40 minutes.

Curried Butternut Squash Soup

Vegetable cooking spray
1 medium onion
1 (1-lb.) butternut squash, peeled and chopped
3 cups water
1/2 tsp. curry powder
1 tsp. chicken or vegetable bouillon cubes (optional)

Spray the cooking spray onto a small pan and saute the onion in it till soft. Add to other ingredients in a medium saucepan. Cover and simmer 30 minutes, or until squash is tender. Remove from heat. Puree in batches in food processor or blender. Good hot or cold.

Vegetable Casserole

1/2 cup uncooked rice
2 cups fresh green beans or lima beans
3 medium baking potatoes
2 medium zucchini or yellow squash
1 large bell pepper
1 large onion
6 cloves garlic
2 medium tomatoes
1 1/2 tsp. salt
1/4 tsp. black pepper
2 Tbsp. fresh dill
1/4 cup fresh parsley, chopped
Dash of garlic powder
1/3 cup olive oil

Sprinkle rice in bottom of 9"x13" pan. Layer beans or limas, potatoes (sliced), squash (sliced into rounds), peppers (chopped), onions and garlic (chopped), and tomatoes (sliced). Season with salt, pepper, garlic powder, dill and parsley. Drizzle oil on top. Cover tightly with foil and bake at 425 degrees for one hour. Remove foil and bake at 375 degrees another 1/2 hour.

Linda Barnes

Linda Barnes, who lives in Brookline, Massachusetts, is author of the Michael Spraggue mysteries, including Bitter Finish *and* Dead Heat. *Her current series of best-selling mysteries, including* Coyote and Snapshot, *feature Carlotta Carlyle.*

Carlotta rarely cooks, but when the spirit moves her, she's been known to make pots, even vats, of chili. It freezes well, and takes the edge off New England winters. It's a free-form recipe. She ladles in the spices with a liberal hand, rarely measuring, prefering the little-bit-of-this, little-bit-of-that tradition of her Jewish grandmother. (Of course, her grandmother would shudder at the *treyf* use of cheese, but Carlotta's no purist.)

Here goes:

Carlotta's Killer Chili

2 lbs. hamburger
1 Tbsp. oil
1 large Spanish onion, diced
6-8 cloves garlic, finely chopped or pressed
About 3 Tbsp. chili powder—more or less is fine; what's important is the two-to-one ratio with the following two ingredients:
About 1-1/2 Tbsp. paprika
About 1-1/2 Tbsp. salt
A few generous shakes of garlic salt
2 #10 cans whole peeled tomatoes, plus 2/3 can of water
1 can Progresso red kidney beans

Saute onions and garlic in oil till translucent. Add and brown hamburger. Add all seasonings. Stir. Add tomatoes, slicing them with the edge of a spatula until roughly chopped. Add water and kidney beans. Bring slowly to a boil, then simmer for 20 minutes. You can make it well in advance and stick it in the fridge. It gets better with reheating. Serving options: Add about 1 cup wide egg noodles cooked. Place a bowl of shredded Montery Jack with jalapeno peppers on the table. Brave guests can spice up the chili to their stomachs' content. Serves 6 or so.

Carlotta and I hope you enjoy this. I tried to talk her into divulging her grandmother's chicken soup recipe, but there are a few things she still holds sacred.

Dave Barry

Dave Barry, Pulitzer Prize winning syndicated columnist for the Miami Herald's Tropic Magazine *is the author of numerous best sellers, including the recent* Dave Barry Is Not Making This Up. *The TV show* "Dave's World" *is loosely based on his life.*

Toast With Peanut Butter

This is a hearty snack that I generally enjoy 30 or 40 times per day when I'm supposed to be writing a column. You get yourself a slice of white bread, the kind with no fiber or vitamins or anything else healthy in it, and you put it in your toaster and push the lever down. I like my toast well-done, so I push the lever down three or four times, until the smoke detector is beeping. Then I get a spoon and smear a fist-size gob of Peter Pan brand peanut butter (creamy, NOT chunky!) on the toast and eat it.

If you're in a hurry, you can skip the toast and put the peanut butter straight into your mouth.

If you're in a REAL hurry, you can also skip the spoon.

Michael Bishop

Michael Bishop, who lives in Pine Mountain, Georgia, is the author of more than 15 books, including the novels, Philip K. Dick Is Dead, Alas, Ancient of Days, *and the 1982 Nebula-Award winner* No Enemy But Time. *His most recent novel, the World War Two baseball fantasy* Brittle Innings, *has been purchased for a film by Twentieth Century Fox. Bishop also has published poetry, criticism, and nonfiction, but prefers concocting recipes on behalf of the characters in his novels.*

Unicorn Mountain, *which won the Mythopoeic Fantasy Award in 1988, features as one of its four protagonists Libby Quarrels, the originator of Cowboy Carrot Chili.*

Libby Quarrels's Cowboy Carrot Chili

1 lb. lean ground beef
1 large onion...I mean LARGE
2 stalks fresh celery
2 small green bell peppers
2 15-oz. cans of peeled crushed tomatoes
2 15-0z. cans of chili-style beans
1 15-0z. can of red kidney beans
2 tsp. chili powder...or more to taste
1 tsp. crushed red peppers...or more, or less, to taste
1 Tbsp. Grandma's Famous Light "Unsulphured" Molasses...or substitute...or not at all
1 large carrot
Salt to taste

Brown ground beef in skillet or in microwave, drain off fat, add to open-topped pressure cooker or crockpot. Add crushed tomatoes, chili beans, and kidney beans to meat. Dice onion, celery, green peppers and add to mixture. Add chili powder, crushed red peppers, salt, and molasses. Grate in whole carrot. Cook on high in crockpot for 4 or 5 hours, perhaps turning down to low for last hour or so. You can use an open pressure cooker on the stovetop at a moderate eye setting for 3 or 4 hours or until the ingredients seem well melded together. Some folks may want to drain the kidney beans before adding them to the pot. A 4th or 5th can of beans, chili or kidney, is not out of the question if you like beans. This is a great dish because you can tinker with it, holding out the green peppers until the last hour, adding a dab of mustard or grape jelly or garlic salt if your taste runs that way. Serves a couple of people for several days or until they can't stand each other any longer. Tastes especially good with corn chips and Mexican beer.

Jerry Bledsoe

Jerry Bledsoe, a former newspaper columnist and contributing editor to Esquire, *is the author of 13 books, including the No. 1 bestseller,* Bitter Blood, *which was made into a mini-series for CBS starring Kelly McGillis, Keith Carradine and Harry Hamlin. His newest true-crime book,* Before He Wakes, *is also being developed as a mini-series by CBS. He lives in Asheboro, North Carolina.*

I had intended offering here by famous recipe for Left-handed Whelk Chowder, which I used to cook every year at the Strange Seafood Festival at the Hampton Mariners Museum in Beaufort, N.C. This dish was rightly famous (featured in *Southern Living* and on the nationally syndicated TV show, *PM Magazine*) and proclaimed by far the best at the festival by all who tasted it, which may not be so great a compliment considering that the other choices ranged from mole crab soup and eel-on-a-spit to steamed marsh snails and sea kale salad.

Alas, though, whelks of all persuasions are verging on becoming endangered, and the already rare left-handed whelk is now almost impossible to find. Therefore, I offer another seafood dish, this one famous only among my friends. I call it Seafood Bledsonia because I once had a dish at an Italian restaurant that the owner had named after himself. His name was Anthony, and he called his dish Seafood Antonia. My dish and his aren't much alike (mine is decidedly superior), but I named mine after his because I just liked the way that "nia" sounded at the end of Bledsoe.

I should warn that this definitely is a "rich" dish, costly to prepare and definitely not for the calorie conscious or cholesterol wary. Please note, too, that I never use measurements when cooking so those offered are only approximations and you are free to tinker with them to suit your own tastes.

Seafood Bledsonia

1 lb. crabmeat (any crab meat will do, but lump, blue crab meat is best)
1/2 lb. shrimp
1/2 lb. scallops (preferably bay scallops)
1/2 lb. firm white fish (grouper or red snapper)
2 lobster tails (preferably Maine lobster, but the tropical so-called lobsters, which really are big crayfish, will do
2 cups rice
1/2 lb. butter
16 oz. clam juice
1 pt. cream
6 Tbsp. flour
1/4 cup sherry
1 large sweet red pepper
1/2 pound Swiss cheese shredded
1/2 pound mozarella cheese shredded
1/2 pound freshly grated parmesan cheese

Steam rice. Roast pepper in oven, remove skin and dice. Remove skin from fish and cut into chunks. Cut lobster tails into chunks. Pick crabmeat to remove all shell and cartilage. Melt 1 stick butter in large sauce pan over low heat so that it doesn't brown. Saute fish, lobster, shrimp, scallops until translucence is gone. Do not overcook. Remove to side dish, leaving butter in pan. Add crabmeat to butter and warm. In another sauce pan, make a roux of flour and the other stick of butter, being careful not to brown it. Slowly add clam juice and cream until sauce has reached a medium-to-heavy thickness. Add sherry. Spread rice to a depth of about 3/4 inch in large baking dish. Cover with seafood, making a good mix. Dot with diced pepper. Pour sauce over this and top with cheeses. Place in 350-degree oven until cheeses begin to brown. One taste and you will sing my praises forever.

Judy Blume

Judy Blume is the author of some of the most popular children's books ever published, including, Are You There, God *and* Here's to You Rachel Robinson. *She has won numerous awards from as far away as Australia and Europe. Her book* Forever... *was made into a movie for TV. She has a son and daughter and divides her time between Connecticut and New York City.*

Twelve years ago I spent a month in Maine, on a small island off Port Clyde. Twice a week we grocery shopped by boat, and always stopped for lunch at a tiny sandwich shop. That's where I first tasted broccoli salad. By the end of the month I convinced the owner of the shop to tell me her secret, which I'm happy to share with you. It's delicious, healthy and tastes a lot better than it sounds (as long as you like broccoli!). It can be made from fresh uncooked or lightly steamed broccoli.

Port Clyde Broccoli Salad Sandwich

1 cup broccoli
1 tsp. (or less) mayonnaise
Juice from a lemon wedge
Salt and pepper to taste

Chop broccoli florets into tiny pieces. (I use a Cuisinart.) Add just enough mayonnaise to keep the salad together. Squeeze in the juice from a wedge of lemon. Add salt and pepper to taste. Mix well. Spread on your favorite kind of bread. Yum!

Larry Bond

After serving in the Navy, Larry Bond collaborated with Tom Clancy on Red Storm Rising *before beginning his own series of military bestsellers, including* Red Phoenix *and* Vortex. *He also creates computerized war games.*

Apple Torte

First Layer:
    1/2 cup butter
    1/3 cup sugar
    1 cup flour
    1/4 tsp. vanilla

Cream butter and sugar together, add vanilla. Blend in the flour and spread on the bottom and sides of a 9" pie pan.

Second Layer:
    1 8-oz. pkg. cream cheese (can use "lite")
    1/4 cup sugar
    1 egg
    1/4 tsp. vanilla

Combine sugar and cheese, add egg and vanilla. Pour into pie pan.

Third Layer:
    1/3 cup sugar
    1/2 tsp. cinnamon
    4 cups peeled, sliced Granny Smith apples
    1/4 cup sliced almonds

Combine all together and arrange in a circle design on top of filling. Bake at 450 degrees for 10 minutes then 400 for 25 minutes. Some people like to put 2 tapioca into the apples. I don't.

Michael Bond

British author and playwright Michael Bond, creator of the enormously popular Paddington Bear series for children, is currently writing a series of adult novels featuring an ex-detective who has become a food inspector, Monsieur Pamplemousse.

I have no idea what the collective noun for a group of French chefs is (a cuisine?), but if you ever come across such a gathering and pose the question: "What do you enjoy cooking for yourself?" the chances are that most of them will plump for something comparatively simple. It is a natural reaction to slaving away all day long over a hot stove. Besides, the grass is always greener....

In the second book of the Monsieur Pamplemousse series—*Monsieur Pamplemousse and the Secret Mission*—my eponymous hero, an ex member of the Paris Surete turned inspector for *Le Guide*, France's oldest culinary bible, finding himself landed with the task of preparing a "simple" meal for the patronne of a small hotel in the Loire opted for *Oeufs 'a la Toupinel*—a dish I recalled reading about first of all in *The Hundred Glories of French Cooking* by Robert Courtine.

Baked Potatoes a la Pamplemousse

Take several large potatoes—preferably of a floury variety—and bake them in a hot oven. Oiling the skins first will accelerate the process and make for a harder, darker outer skin.
While they are cooking prepare the filling: some minced lean ham, eggs for poaching—one for each potato—butter, cream, nutmeg, salt, breadcrumbs, grated Parmesan cheese, and the ingredients for making a Mornay sauce. (The latter should be prepared at the

last moment).

When the potatoes are ready, take a sharp knife and remove a lengthways slice from each. Scoop out the inside and mash it in a bowl, adding butter, cream, a pinch of salt and a little grated nutmeg to taste.

Replace the potato inside the skins, leaving a cavity in the centre of each, into which you then place 1 tsp. of Mornay sauce, a little minced ham and a well-drained poached egg. Top it with more sauce, followed by a sprinkling of breadcrumbs and grated cheese. Add a few drops of melted butter and place it back in the oven to brown.

Sauce Mornay

If you look up Sauce Mornay in Escoffier's *Ma Cuisine*, the opening words are: to one pint of cream bechamel sauce (see page 23) add... Turn to page 23 and what do you find? To make two pints of cream béchamel sauce, take 3-1/2 oz. light brown roux (see page 18)... all of which is rather daunting and by now the potatoes will be starting to smoke.

In the book, Monsier Pamplemousse took the easy way out. He did all the enjoyable bits himself and then called on the *patronne* to provide the sauce: "While I am gone you could perhaps prepare me a Sauce Mornay if it isn't too much trouble." No doubt most professional chefs would do likewise.

Those less skilled in the gentle art of sauce-making may like to take the easy way out. Buy a packet of ready-to-mix béchamel sauce. When it is almost ready to boil add to it a mixture of 2 lightly beaten egg yolks and a little cream. Stirring continuously, add 2 tbsp. of butter and a slightly larger amount of grated parmesan cheese and combine. Use immediately.

Rick Boyer

A former editor at Little, Brown, Rick Boyer joined David Savageau to publish the first Places Rated Almanac *in 1982. Boyer also is the author of a series of novels featuring Doc Adams, an oral surgeon who solves murders. One of those novels won an Edgar Award in 1983. Boyer's first novel,* The Giant Rat of Sumatra, *originally published in 1976, was recently reissued by Armchair Detective Press.*

One of the tastiest and most beneficial fish you can buy is fresh salmon. Here's a way to prepare it in a few minutes that will keep your kitchen odor-free and will delight your family and guests.

Doc's Baked Salmon with 3-C's Sauce

Salmon filets or steaks (either one). As many as you like—this recipe can make as much as you want. Make sure the fish is absolutely fresh. Sniff them; there should be no heavy odor. Examine them; they should be bright orange-red and shiny wet.

1. Smear each piece of fish with enough high-quality mayonnaise (Hellman's is best) to coat it liberally, bottom, top, and sides. You should see no red fish through the mayo.
2. Slice a lemon or two crosswise into thin slices. The slice should be thin enough so you can read a printed page through them. Use a sharp knife to do this. Place as many lemon slices on each steak/filet as will fit. Then sprinkle with fresh Hungarian paprika and fresh-ground black pepper.
3. Place fish on baking sheet or ovenproof glass and put on top rack of oven preheated at 400 degrees. Do not turn down oven.

4. While the fish is baking—it should take 10-15 minutes, no more, unless the pieces are very thick—make the "3-C's" sauce as follows:

Ingredients: mayonnaise, cumin, curry, and capers (hence the name: 3 C's...if you haven't figured it out yet...).
Proportions: for each cup of mayonnaise, add 1tbsp. each of cumin and curry (more or less to taste), and about 1/4 to 1/3 cup of drained capers. Again, proportions are a matter of taste. Mix together. Additional options: juice of 1/2 lemon, 1tsp. Dijon mustard.
When the salmon is baked (it will flake nicely with a fork), remove it from oven. SURPRISE! You were worried about all that sloppy mayo on the salmon, weren't you? Well, guess what? It's gone! Actually, it has melted into the fish, enhancing its flavor and keeping it super moist. Serve with the sauce and additional lemon wedges on the side. This dish is a winner! Easy to make, quick, and perfect for any time of year. Clean up is a snap.

—Doc Adams

T. Coraghessan Boyle

T. Coraghessan Boyle, who teaches at the University of Southern California, has been published in many magazines, including Esquire, Paris Review, Atlantic Monthly and Harpers. *His novels have won wide acclaim. They include* East is East, The Road to Wellville, *and* Water Music.

[Excerpted from *Water Music.*]

One evening he witnessed a wedding. It was strikingly similar to the funeral he'd attended: keening hags, howling dogs, a solemn procession. The bride was a walking shroud, veiled from head to foot, even her eyes invisible. He wondered how she was able to see where she was going. The keening women followed her, their stride measured by the beat of a tabala. The groom wore slippers with upturned toes. He was accompanied by a retinue of Mussulmen in embroidered burnooses and a cordon of slaves leading goats and bullocks, and carrying a tent. At an appointed spot the tent was struck, the goats and bullocks slaughtered, a fire ignited in a depression in the earth. There was a feast. Beef and mutton, songbirds, roasted larvae and other delicacies. There was dancing, songs were sung and tales told. And then there was the piece de resistance: a whole baked camel.

Baked Camel (Stuffed)

500 dates
200 plover eggs
20 two-pound carp

4 bustards, cleaned and plucked
2 sheep
1 large camel
Seasonings

Dig trench. Reduce inferno to hot coals, th3ree feet in depth. Separately hard-cook eggs. Scale carp and stuff with shelled eggs and dates. Season bustards and stuff with stuffed carp. Stuff stuffed bustards into sheep and stuffed sheep into camel. Singe camel. Then wrap in leaves of doum palm and bury in pit. Bake two days. Serve with rice. Serves 400.

Bill Bozzone

A playwright and screenwriter, Bill Bozzone won the 1994 Eugene O'Neill Playwriting Competition. His credits include the screenplay for the feature film Full Moon in Blue Water *which starred Gene Hackman, Teri Garr, and Burgess Meredith. He co-wrote the TNT network feature* The Last Elephant, *which starred James Earl Jones. He is on the faculty of The Writer's Voice Project in Manhattan.*

This is Floyd's (played by Gene Hackman) recipe from the Blue Water Cafe. Served with a Lone Star Texas Longneck beer, of course. (To see the Blue Water Cafe, you can rent *Full Moon in Blue Water* at your local video store.)

Floyd's Crab Cakes

1 lb. fresh backfin or lump crab meat
2 eggs lightly beaten
2-1/2 Tbsp. mayonnaise
1 tsp. dijon mustard
1/4 cup diced green pepper, sauted briefly in butter
2 slices of bread, slightly stale
1 tsp. Worcestershire sauce
1-1/2 tsp. parsley
1/2 tsp. Old Bay seasoning

Mix ingredients with exception of crab meat thoroughly. Fold in crab meat that has been picked carefully for shells. Shape into six cakes. Refrigerate for one hour minimum. Place under broiler until lightly browned, turning once.

Lilian Jackson Braun

All 11 of Lilian Jackson Braun's bestselllng The Cat Who... novels are still in print. She lives in the mountains of North Carolina with her husband and two cats, Koko and Pitti Sing, both Siamese.

[From Plots and Pans: Recipes and Antidotes From the Mystery Writers of America.]

Pork Liver Cupcakes (for Felines)

1 lb. pork liver
1/4 cup salad oil
1/2 cup wheat germ
Rolled oats

Open doors and windows. Turn on ventilating fan. Simmer liver in water to cover until tender and repulsively gray. Place in blender with oil, wheat germ and enough rolled oats to make a yukky paste. Freeze individual servings in paper muffin cups. Thaw and remove from paper. Garnish with caviar or whatever. Yield: 12 or more servings (for cats, that is).

This recipe was developed by the late Antoine Delapierre, chef at the Old Stone Mill in Pickax, for his proposed line of "Fabulous Frozen Foods for Fussy Felines." Readers of *The Cat Who Knew Shakespeare* are aware that the line was never marketed.

Sue Ellen Bridgers

Although Sue Ellen Bridgers' books, which include Notes From Another Life *and* Keeping Christina, *are generally classified as being for young adults, they appeal to all ages.* Bridgers has won the Boston Globe *Horn Book Award and received two American Book Award nominations. She has also been published in* Redbook, Ingenue, and Carolina Quarterly.

Artichoke Rice Salad

1 pkg. chicken Rice-a-Roni
4 chopped green onions
1/2 cup chopped bell pepper
2 jars (6 oz.) marinated artichokes with juice, chopped
3/4 tsp. curry powder
1/2 cup slivered almonds

Make Rice-a-Roni according to pkg. directions. Cool. Add other ingredients and refrigerate for 8 hours. Garnish with tomatoes, cucumber and avocado slices, if desired.

Dr. Joyce Brothers

In addition to being a columnist for newspapers and magazines, as well as host of TV and radio shows, Psychologist Joyce Brothers is the author of numerous books, including Widowed *and* What Every Woman Should Know About Men. *An excerpt from her newest book,* Positive Plus: A Practical Plan for Liking Yourself Better, *was published in* Parade Magazine.

Meat Loaf

2 cups fresh bread crumbs
3/4 cup minced onion
1/4 minced green pepper
2 eggs
2 lbs. chuck, ground
2 Tbsp. horseradish
2-1/2 tsp. salt
1 tsp. dry mustard
1/4 cup milk or evaporated milk
3/4 cup catchup

1. When it's convenient, prepare bread crumbs, minced onion, green pepper.
2. About one hour before serving start heating oven to 400 degrees.
3. In large bowl, with fork, beat eggs slightly. Lightly mix in chuck, then crumbs, onion, pepper. (Meat will be juicier and more tender if you handle it as little as possible.) Add horseradish, salt, mustard, milk, 1/4 cup catchup. Combine lightly but well.

4. In bowl, shape meat into oval loaf; transfer to shallow baking dish or broil-and-serve platter; smooth into shapely loaf. Spread top with 1/2 cup catchup. Bake 50 min.

5. Serve from baking dish or broil-and-serve platter, pouring off excess juices. Or, with 2 broad spatulas, lift loaf out of baking dish onto heated platter. Spoon some of juices over meat. (Nice chilled, then served sliced, too.) Makes 8 servings.

P.S. If you prefer a soft, moist exterior, bake meat loaf as directed, in 9"x5"x3" loaf pan. Pour juices from pan after baking. Unmold meat loaf onto cake rack; then place, right side up, on heated platter. Use juices for making gravy if desired.

Rosellen Brown

Rosellen Brown, whose novels include Before and After *and* Civil Wars, *received a Guggenheim Fellowship and a Woodrow Wilson Fellowship. Her short fiction has been included several times in* O. Henry Prize Stories *and* Best American Short Stories *and she's been published in* Ms, Atlantic Monthly *and* Hudson Review.

Now that *Like Water For Chocolate* has entranced the world—and yes, those fried green tomatoes, too—I'm happy to ante up a favorite for you. Unfortunately, though I like food all too much, my characters don't talk about it as much as they might, let alone offer recipes. True, in my recent novel *Before and After*, Ben speaks about making a good red snapper Veracruzana, and he serves chili at a climactic moment, but neither of those recipes seems quite right. Here's one I love, though, and find endlessly useful, even if it hasn't aided the love lives of my characters or seen them through bad days in the kitchen. (In that novel, faced by a crisis, I have to admit my fictional family resorts, pathetically, to canned tomato soup and chocolate pudding. Ah well. Not everyone can be M. F. K. Fisher, and who knows what she did when things got really dreary?)

The One Necessary (Satay) Sauce

1/2 cup soy sauce, mixed with as much molasses as you need to sweeten it to your liking
1 tsp. cayenne pepper
3/4 cup hot water
1/3 cup peanut butter

1/2 cup roasted peanuts, ground (you can use all peanut butter, crunchy; real peanuts give it more texture)
 1 clove garlic, minced
 Juice of one lemon, or 1 capful bottled lemon juice

You can also reserve some of this and add about 1/2 can tomato sauce, a little more water and more lemon juice; heat it up with more cayenne or tabasco and serve it as extra sauce on the side. I use this on chicken or beef or lamb. You can use it wonderfully on fish, on vegetables like potatoes, rice, pasta—really just about anything. Make it as mild or as hot as you like it.

Algis Budrys

Algis Budrys, whose parents brought him to this country from Lithuania, has been editor-in-chief of Regency Books and editorial director of Playboy Press. He has written hundreds of stories and articles as well as many science fiction novels, including Rogue Moon *and* Falling Torch. *He is book review editor for* Fantasy and Science Fiction *magazine and editor of the annual* L. Ron Hubbard Presents Writers of the Future *anthology.*

Coaster Pancakes

Take 1 egg per person. Separate eggs and set whites aside. Combine yolks with enough milk and flour to make a batter with the consistency of enamel paint. Add salt to taste.

Take an iron frying pan of the appropriate size and build a fire under it, letting it heat thoroughly while you whip the egg whites stiff.

Combine the batter and the egg whites.

Bring the batter, a soup ladle, and lots of butter to the immediate vicinity of the frying pan. Put a lot of butter in the frying pan and pour pancakes into the pan, each pancake to be about 2" in diameter. Pour as many pancakes as you have room for. Fry until the center of the pancake is golden brown, with a crisp, raised edge that is a frank brown.

Repeat until all the batter is gone. Serve with sour cream.

Eat. Lie down.

It will probably take you a little practice until you get everything right. You will find that all but the grossest failures are delicious. Cholesterol? In Lithuania, they never heard of cholesterol.

Orson Scott Card

Orson Scott Card's science fiction novels, which include The Call of Earth *and* Lost Boys, *have won great acclaim. He won both the Hugo and Nebula awards two years running. Also a playwright, he has been director of his own theater company. A native of Utah, where he grew up in the Mormon Church and was graduated from Brigham Young University, he spent his missionary years in Brazil, where he learned to speak fluent Portugese andtook a liking to the cooking.*

Feijoada is a popular Brazilian dish. This is an Americanized version.

American Feijoada

Rinse 2 cups black beans in cold water. Place in crock pot with 5 cups cold water. Remove all floating debris. Soak beans for 10-12 hours. Do not drain water. Add:

Leek or onion, chopped, about 1/2 cup to 1 cup (to taste)
Fresh cilantro, chopped, 1/8 cup
1 can stewed tomatoes (including juices). Burst tomatoes with spoon so they don't stay whole during cooking
1 pkg.powdered taco seasoning mix (Ortega)
1-2 tsp. chili powder
2-3 tsp. cinnamon
1 tsp. lemon pepper
1 tsp. tarragon
1/2 tsp. garlic powder

3 dashes savory
3 dashes powdered thyme
1/4 tsp. salt
1/2 an eye of round roast or 1/2 a london broil, diced to 1/2-3/4 inch cubes (trim any fat)

Cook in crock pot on high 6-8 hours or on low 12-16 hours. One hour before end of cooking, add 1 can drained pineapple (cubed) or mandarin oranges. Serve over rice.

Optional: top serving with cheese, chopped lettuce and tomato, avocado.

Warning: juice of black beans will stain a permanent deep purple.

Ron Carlson

Both of Ron Carlson's story collections, Plan B for the Middle Class *and* The News of the World *were selected by the* New York Times *to be among the best books of the year. Also the author of two novels, Carlson has received a National Endowment of the Arts Fellowship and was the winner of the 1993* Ploughshares *Cohen Prize for fiction. He is director of creative writing at Arizona State University.*

First of all, they're not dinghies, but I'm not calling them canoes, boats, dories, or gondolas. I was tempted to go with gondola, but the truth is the salad dish I'm going to describe doesn't look like a gondola, and the word itself can be tricky, I mean, is it gon-dola or gond-ola, and given all the other questions this entree is bound to engender, you're not going to need people looking down their noses at those who pronounce gondola the wrong way (whichever that is) as they ask for seconds or thirds. It's going to be hard enough for some to say, "May I have another dinghy?" But at least they won't be in danger of an elocution faux pas. Anyway this recipe is called Rice-a-Roni Avocado Dinghies and here is how it is prepared.

Rice-a-Roni Avocado Dinghies

One pkg. Rice-a-Roni (any flavor)
Avocados (one each for each cup of Rice-a-Roni)
One head of fresh lettuce
Cherry tomatoes

Prepare Rice-a-Roni as pkg. directs, simmering 15 minutes. Place in a bowl in refrigerator all day or overnight. Just before dinner set avocado halves on lettuce leaves on a salad plate. Fill each avocado with a scoop of your chilled Rice-a-Roni. Garnish with 1 or 2 tomatoes.

This can be a salad course or a light late supper. I like it because it's a sure conversation starter. I mean, many of your guests will not have seen Rice-a-Roni in person before in their lifetimes. "What is this delicious chilled rice-vermicelli salad?" they'll ask. Well, it's Rice-a-Roni. But what is Rice-a-Roni anyway? It's more than rice and vermicelli. It's the San Francisco Treat. Check the box near the little red and yellow cable car at the top. "The San Francisco Treat." Think of it, a city with its own treat. Are there other cities with a rice dish? I don't think so. The Chicago Treat? The Atlanta Treat? The Des Moines Treat? And your dinner is off and running from there. Possible conversation starters: Have you ever been to San Francisco? Have you ever ridden on a cable car? What do you think the future of public transportation might be? Do you know the history of avocado farming? Did you ever have a neighbor who was gifted with the ability to plant and foster an avocado seed until the plant dominated the kitchen with its sad green light as you drank coffee together years ago when you were young?

Fred Chappell

Fred Chappell, who teaches at the University of North Carolina at Greensboro is the recipient of the Bollingen Prize in Poetry, the Award in Literature from the National Institute of Arts and Letters, and the T. S. Eliott Award. His novels include Dagon *and* Brighten the Corner Where You Are.

The characters Joe Robert Kirkman and his wife Cora inhabit a couple of novels I published: *I Am One of You Forever* and *Brighten the Corner Where You Are*. They hold quite different philosophies of life, as their respective cornbread recipes illustrate.

Joe Robert's Fishing Cabin Cornbread

Get the wood range good and hot and fry up some bacon. Take out the bacon when it's as crisp as new money and pour off a fair amount of the grease. Keep that in a coffee can for greasing boots. Stop dogs from chewing boots.
Cut up some little green onions, tops and all, and watch them sizzle a few minutes in the pan.
Meanwhile, be making your batter—some buttermilk, about a full drinking glass of it, four handfuls white cornmeal, salt, plenty of red or black pepper, baking powder, about a spoonful, maybe less. Put all this into a quart Mason jar. Add an egg if you like but be careful breaking. Bits of shell add texture but alarm females. Screw the top on the jar and shimmy like a Ford truck with a shot wheel bushing.
Pour batter out on top of the onions unless they're burned too much by now. A little black doesn't hurt; kind of sweet, in fact. Put in oven and add firewood to firebox.

Eat when ready with butter and country ham and black coffee with molasses sweetening.

Utter thanksgiving and pray for mercy.

Cora's Cornbread Delight

Clean up kitchen and wash dishes if Joe Robert has been messing about.

- 1-1/2 cup yellow cornmeal
- 1/2 cup cake flour
- 1 Tbsp. sugar
- 2 tsp. baking powder
- 1 tsp. baking soda
- 2 eggs, though Eggbeaters make a lighter batter and prettier bread
- 1-1/2 cup buttermilk
- 1 cup fresh corn sliced from cob; add cob juice
- 1-1/2 cups grated extra sharp cheddar cheese
- 2-3 scallions sliced thin, some green included

Grease an ordinary biscuit pan, 15"x10". Sift cornmeal, flour, sugar, baking powder, salt, and soda into one bowl; in the other beat the buttermilk and eggs. Add the dry to the wet and stir till mixed, but not thoroughly. Pour into pan and spread smooth. Bake in middle of 425 degree oven for about 15 minutes.

Remove and cool on racks. Find a place to hide it until suppertime or passers-through will keep breaking off pieces till nothing is left. Make sure cat doesn't find hiding place.

Suzy McKee Charnas

Once a Peace Corps volunteer in Nigeria, Suzy McKee Charnas is a devoted researcher who familiarizes herself with everything from crude plastics to nomadic stock herders to ensure authenticity in her science fiction books, which include The Kingdom of Kevin Malone *and* The Golden Thread. *She is the recipient of a Nebula Award.*

Jacob's Guile

1-1/2 cups lentils
1 tsp. salt
2 cups chopped onions
1 tsp. salt
1/4 cup olive oil
3/4 cups brown rice and water to cook
1-1/2 Tbsp. butter

Soak lentils in cold water 2 hours before cooking. Drain, put in a pot with 1 tsp. salt and 2 cups fresh cold water, bring to boil and let simmer.
Meantime heat 1/4 cup olive oil in a frying pan, add 2 cups chopped onions and 1 tsp. salt. Cook slowly, covered, until onions are soft and yellow (about 5 minutes).
Wash 3/4 cup brown rice and drain. Melt 1-1/2 Tbsp. butter in a small skillet, turn up heat and parch rice in butter, stirring constantly till rice goes from transluscent to opaque white.
Add rice and onion to the lentils plus 1/2 cup extra water and cook slowly, covered, till rice is done.
Serve with salad (lettuce, tomato, onion, oil and vinegar is best),

dished out with or even right on top of portions of Guile (the combination is unbelievably delicious).

If you take Jacob's Guile to a potluck don't be surprised if it just sits there getting cold. It is not sexy-looking and will not mesmerize people—unless they taste it, in which case they are lost. Guile is reputed to be the very food (a "mess of pottage") for which Esau gave up his birthright to the advantage of his clever brother Jacob in the Old Testament (hence the name of the dish). Try some and discover a new respect for Esau, who otherwise appears to be not only "an hairy man" but a birdbrain.

Personally, I think that if you could get a vampire to taste Jacob's Guile, he or she would at once expire out of sheer envy of us ordinary folk who (perhaps as compensation for our dinky little life spans) can feast on such divine fare.

C. J. Cherryh

C. J. Cherryh has written more than 30 books, including Chanur's Legacy *and* Yvgenie, *and has won three Hugo Awards. One of the most prolific and respected science fiction writers, she likes to explore "the theme of absolute power, especially when held by a woman, and the theme of culture as a force shaping the whole of life."*

Although all my characters are fond of eating, few actually like to cook. In fact, the only one I can think of who really likes it is a character from a book which won't appear for another year. And he likes to bake (which I don't do).

Diced Chicken with Carrot/Mustard Sauce and Rice
(copyright 1994 by C.J. Cherryh)

Grill chicken. (If you don't have a grill, cook in separate skillet and poach in wine and water with lid on to make steam. This also works.) Boil rice: don't use that quickie stuff. Real white rice takes 20 minutes; so does cooking the chicken, and it tastes better. Brown takes 30 minutes. (Cooking real rice: In either case, the ratio is one cup rice for 2 people, 2 cups water. Bring water to boil, add dry rice, cover, bring back to boil, immediately reduce heat to extreme low, leave lid on for 20 minutes.)

For sauce: 2 Tbsp. brown mustard, in skillet, with diced fresh carrots, plus 1 Tbsp. whole-grain-with-wine type mustard—this is often imported from France, is called Engrained Mustard with Wine, and if you can't get it, increase the brown mustard 1 Tbsp. Add dusting of curry powder, cognac, 1 Tbsp. parsley. Add 1 pat real butter. Allow butter to brown, even burn; 1 Tbsp. brown sugar, water, keep going on low heat until chicken is done. Any time it starts to burn, add more water, but it should stay just a little more watery than the mustard at most moments. Dice grilled chicken. Add to mustard sauce.

Add salt, black pepper, dried basil, cooked rice and stir.

Add 1 Tbsp. corn starch to quarter cup warm water, add to mustard sauce, increase heat to high until it generates enough sauce for rice.

Pour sauce and chicken over rice.

Serve side of green vegetables.

Amy Clampitt

A former book editor, Amy Clampitt has been a Guggenhein Fellow and is a winner of the Bernice Kavinoky Isaacson Award for Poetry. Her books include Westward *and* Predecessors Etcetera.

Fresh, bright-green spinach, too young and beautiful to be cooked, deserves a salad to itself, unencumbered by the fatty bacon bits, the croutons, the limp mushrooms, or the gummy commercial dressing by which it would be overpowered in the usual restaurant version. Here is the way I dress it.

Spinach Vinaigrette

1/2 tsp salt
1/4 tsp. freshly ground black pepper
Scant 1/4 tsp. dry mustard
1 Tbsp. good red wine vinegar
1 Tbsp. olive oil

Blend salt, pepper and mustard; add vinegar, let stand a minute or two; stir vigorously, making sure the salt is dissolved; add olive oil, and stir or shake vigorously until well blended. Pour over and toss briefly with:

A generous bunch of young spinch, carefully washed and trimmed
1 small sweet red pepper, sliced
Part of a small red onion, sliced

If available, a handful of fresh dill, loosely pulled apart shredded carrot, thinly sliced celery, and Boston lettuce are tasty additions or substititons. Serves 2 to 4.

Terry Cline

Terry Cline has been a comedy writer and syndicated columnist. His novels include Damon, Reaper *and* Missing Persons. *He is now developing a TV comedy series.*

This is a sinful, but healthy-as-can-be-expected-with-pecans recipe. Not to worry though. Eat sparingly. It beats any fiber-based or natural oil remedy for what ails you—and umm-mmm, they are so good!

Terry Cline's Lowest Cholesterol Roasted Pecans

2 cups of shelled pecans
2 Tbsp. canola oil
Salt

Preheat oven to 350 degrees. Put shelled pecans into a container that can be capped, and add canola oil. Turn the container repeatedly until the pecans are uniformly oiled. Spread the nuts on a cookie sheet, being careful not to heap them. Use a cookie pan with sides so excess oil won't drip in the oven. Salt liberally. Roast for 25 minutes; shake the pan to be certain the nuts are not sticking, then roast another 5 minutes or until slightly browned. Remember, they always taste better after cooling.

Bernard Cornwell

A TV and newspaper journalist in England before moving to this country, Bernard Cornwell is author of the popular Sharpe series of adventure stories set during the Peninsular War in 1808-14, which culminated in Waterloo, *Sharpe's final adventure. Several of these novels have been filmed for television. He has also written contemporary suspense thrillers.*

These recipes are both much used and therefore well tested and genuinely delicious.

The first is a classic French country dish to which I have given an honest English name, though you may, if you wish to impress your guests, call it something like *terrine de porc*. But in whatever language it is cooked, this is a delicious, rich and splendid dish that is ideal for a winter's night. I use the word "rich" deliberately, for this is a recipe that will horrify food-faddists, vegetarians, health-nuts and all those other killjoys who would have us go to our grave upon a diet of twigs, nuts and soybean offal. This is real food. It is also remarkably, even deceptively, easy to cook and should thus be a part of every bachelor's repertoire. Upon marriage, of course, the sensible man relinquishes all cooking duties to his wife, thus managing to offend the feminists as well as the aforementioned food-faddists, etc.

Pig'n'Potato

To serve 4 people (or 2 very hungry people) you will need:

4 large pork chops. If you have a friendly butcher you may

be able to acquire center-cut pork chops which still retain the attached kidneys. Use them if you can find them, but I must confess that in 15 years of living in America I never have. Congress probably made a law about it.

1-1/2 lbs. of potatoes. As I write Washington has just decreed that from now on we are to use metric units. Maybe it's the water there.

1 large onion

4 cloves of garlic

4 Juniper berries. These are difficult to find, so difficult that I buy them whenever I see them and now have a drawerful of juniper berries. If you cannot find the berries, make the dish anyway and add 1 Tbsp. of gin instead. Gin is flavored with juniper berries, and though the addition of the liquor will achieve very little for the taste of the dish it does not hurt either.

4 oz. ham or fat bacon

1 bottle dry white wine or hard cider. You can use alcohol-free 'cider' (i.e. apple juice). but as we pass through this vale of tears but once, why?

Pork dripping. You don't have any, do you? And you can't buy it either. So either make some by collecting the fat drippings from your next pork roast, or else substitute butter

Half pt. thick cream. This is optional.

What you do: You begin by making a slit in each pork chop, close to the bone, and placing therein 1 clove of garlic and 1 juniper berry. Then brown the pork chops in the pork dripping. They're not being cooked at this point, merely heat sealed, so do it quickly on a high heat, then set the chops aside. If you are using butter and find that you burn the butter on high heat then add a drop or 2 of olive oil. This prevents the butter burning.

Peel your potatoes. Slice them thinly. Peel the onion, slice it thinly. Place HALF the potato slices in layers at the bottom of a deep, thick, oven-proof casserole. The nature of this casserole is quite important; it must be robust, and must have a lid. Place the browned pork chops on top of the potato layer. Place the onion on top of the pork chops, add the rest of the potato slices, then add a final layer of the ham (or bacon). Add a scattering of salt and pepper.

Now comes the moment when bravery and a trust in the ineluctable processes of cooking are necessary. You are going to add the liquid, and because your casserole is deep and well stuffed with food, you will be tempted to ignore my instructions and add more than 1 glass of wine. So do it. But if you have faith, and want to see a miracle, add 1 glass of dry white wine or hard cider only. So what, you ask, is the rest of the white wine and cider for? To drink while you are cooking, of course.

Now seal the pot. Do not just place the lid on, but seal it. I generally place 2 or 3 sheets of either greaseproof paper or aluminum foil on the pot then cram the lid on. You have to prevent the steam escaping, otherwise the miracle cannot occur. Put in a pre-heated oven (325 degrees) for 3 hours. It is now, almost, ready. When you take the casserole from the oven you will find that your single glass of wine has miraculously become a rich deep juice enveloping the food. You will also find some excess fat on the surface that you skim away before serving.

The cream is optional, but you might like to experiment by ladling some of the juice into a shallow pan, mixing it with the cream, then reducing the mixture over a very high heat. Then add it back to the meat. This is not really necessary, though the cream does add a delicious taste.

Serve the terrine with a dutiful vegetable. A dutiful vegetable is unobtrusive and easy to cook, like frozen peas. Do NOT serve a salad; you do not want to take up stomach space with ghastly green stuff when you have this casserole to eat. Drink a good red wine with the terrine, or else a good quality ale.

The next is a classic English dish, utterly delicious, simple to make, filling, and satisfyingly offensive to those who preach to us that "we are what we eat" then sit down to platefuls of rabbit food.

I have no explanation for the name which goes back at least 200 hundred years, while the dish itself, like bouillabaisse or gazpacho, belongs to those recipes which have been elevated into classics even though their origins were to serve as a convenient means of using up leftovers. In this case the leftovers would have been scraps of meat.

Toad in the Hole is simply meat in Yorkshire Pudding, and I know of recipes using kidneys, lamb chops and even steak, but the standard meat now used is the British banger. The British banger is a much maligned sausage; it is criticized by ignorant foreigners on the grounds that it contains more fat and bread-crumbs than pork, and the foreigners might well be right, yet they over look one simple truth; the thing tastes wonderful. Yet the thing is also difficult to find in America, and even when it is available it is often too well made here, with too much meat and not enough sawdust, but we must take life as it is given to us, so use pork sausages or breakfast sausages, as large as you can find them. Pennsylvanian scrapple would probably be a wonderful substitute for bangers.

Toad in the Hole

To serve 4 people you will need:

1-1/2 lbs. of sausages
3/4 cup of flour
3/4 cup of milk
1/4 cup of beer
2 eggs

What you do: Sift the flour into a bowl. Add a pinch of salt. Add the milk slowly, beating all the while with a spoon. Then add the beer. You will have had to open a whole bottle to secure a quarter cup, so drink the rest. Whisk the eggs in a separate bowl until they are frothy, then add them to your mix of flour, milk and beer. Beat the new mixture thoroughly, then let it stand in the refrigerator for a half hour.

While the batter is cooling, turn the oven up to 450 degrees. Then fry your sausages, preferably in beef-drippings, but failing that, in butter. Prick the sausages first, to prevent them from exploding, then fry them good and proper until they are dark brown and crispy. Discard most of the hot fat, but keep enough (say half a cup) to cover the bottom of the flat, oven-proof dish in which you will cook the Toad.

Place the fat in the dish, and the dish in the oven. The trick of good Yorkshire Pudding is to have the fat very hot when you add the batter, so place your dish in the oven and leave it there for 10 minutes. If you are using butter and you are afraid the butter will burn, then add a drop or two of olive oil.

Take the heated dish from the oven. Place the cooked sausages in the dish, then pour the batter over the sausages. Put the dish back in the oven and cook at 450 for 15 minutes, then reduce the temperature to 350 and leave the Toad there for another 15 minutes, by which time the batter should have risen and turned golden brown. Try very hard not to keep opening the oven door to check on the progress; it doesn't help.

And that is all there is to it, except to eat it, of course. You can serve it with potatoes and gravy, or eat it by itself, or even eat it cold. Children like the dish, maybe because of its name, or maybe because it is the sort of food they can play with, but if you disapprove of children playing with their food, then you are probably the sort of person who should have neither Toad in the Hole nor children.

Patricia D. Cornwell

Patricia Daniels Cornwell's first novel, Postmortem, *featuring Dr. Kay Scarpetta, Virginia's chief medical examiner, is the only novel ever to win the Edgar, Creasey, Anthony, and Macavity awards, as well as the French Prix du Roman d'Aventure in one year. The subsequent novels featuring Dr. Scarpetta that have followed have become immense international bestsellers. The most recent is* Body Farm.

This is one of Scarpetta's favorite dishes.

Scarpetta's Stew

4 lbs. lean ground sirloin or round steak (or turkey)
3 lbs. lean veal, diced
2 lbs. fresh mushrooms, sliced
1 lb. fresh asparagus, cut in segments
1 lb. fresh small carrots, diced
4 large baking potatoes, peeled and diced
4 large onions, peeled and diced
Bunch of celery, diced 4 bell peppers, red and green, diced
1 or 2 bags fresh spinach
2 whole garlics, crushed
Add any other vegetable you love—broccoli, cauliflower, etc.
1/2 cup virgin olive oil 3 large cans crushed tomatoes
1/2 gallon red wine (burgundy or chianti)
2 quarts V-8 Juice
Salt, pepper, oregano, basil, crushed red pepper to taste

Heat oven to 325 degrees. Heat olive oil in a large skillet and saute meat until lightly brown. Combine with all ingredients in a very large turkey-roaster pan with a cover. If overflow threatens, use an extra pan. Cover and roast stew for at least 5 hours. Then, if desired, reduce heat to 275 and simmer all day. Stir a couple of times during cooking, just to blend. Serve in bowls with hot, crusty Italian bread. Enough for a party of 15 or more.

Janet Dailey

A prolific romance writer, Janet Dailey is one of the world's top-selling authors. For years she was the only American writer for Harlequin. Her more recent books include the four-volume, multi-generational Calder series which was made into a TV miniseries.

This is one of my favorite recipes.

Cupboard Fresh Dressing

1 medium onion, grated
3/4 cup sugar
1 tsp. salt
1/4 tsp. pepper
1/4 tsp. paprika
1 cup vegetable oil
3/4 cup catsup
1/2 cup vinegar

Combine all ingredients in a screw-top jar; shake well. Refrigerate to store. Makes 3-1/2 cups.

Barbara D'Amato

Barbara D'Amato has written musical comedies and worked as a criminal investigator in addition to writing acclaimed mystery novels and true crime books. Her novel, On My Honor, *was nominated for an Anthony in 1990 and* The Doctor, The Murder, The Mystery *won the Agatha in 1994 for best nonfiction.*

My detective, Cat Marsala, is part Italian, and received this recipe from her grandmother. Cat works as a freelance investigative reporter—not a way to get rich, and a sure way to have zero free time. This is surprisingly fast, assuming you can find fresh basil. If you can't, don't make it. It's only good when fresh basil is in season.

Pasta al Pesto

1 pkg. of pasta or an equivalent amount of fresh pasta —enough to serve four (Cat likes to use curly pasta like radiattore or klops because they hold onto the sauce)
1/3 to 1/2 cup olive oil
1 tsp. of black pepper
2 tsp. salt
3 cloves of garlic, more or less, chopped
2 handfuls (or is it handsfull?) FRESH basil
Parmesan or Romano cheese

Boil the pasta according to instructions in lightly salted water. While it's boiling, take the stems and any coarse parts off the basil and put it in a blender with the olive oil, garlic, pepper, and 1 tsp. of salt, more if you like a lot of salt. Blend, but not until it loses all texture. You may buzz it up with a hand-held blender too or anything else that chops thoroughly. Put the basil mixture in a bowl. Rinse and drain the pasta. Toss with the basil. When thoroughly tossed, start sprinkling on grated cheese, and keep adding and tossing to taste. If you add it all at once, it's likely to clump. Serve immediately. It's a nice side dish with a not-too-delicate fish, or with fruit can be a whole lunch or dinner.

Cat's grandmother blends pignolia (pine nuts) into the sauce. Cat doesn't. She doesn't like them. Some people also blend in parsley.
Enjoy.

Charles de Lint

A Canadian, Charles de Lint writes for adults and young readers and regularly has short fiction in The Year's Best Fantasy, Pulphouse, *and the* Borderland *anthologies. His books include* Into the Green *and* Dreams Underfoot. *He also has written horror novels as Samuel M. Key, and is a reviewer, small press publisher and a musician specializing in Celtic folk music.*

This is one of those recipes that is extremely simple to make, yet tastes great as a breakfast, dinner, whatever—depending on how much you like the ingredients, perhaps. But be brave; let me assure you that this combination is a winner, even if you think you don't like either broccoli or feta cheese. Exact measurements aren't really required.

Broccoli & Feta Omelet

What you need are:
- Eggs
- Milk
- Broccoli
- Feta cheese
- Pepper

Steam some broccoli for about 7 minutes (including the time it takes for the water to start to boil). At the same time beat the eggs in a mixing bowl with a small dollop of milk until fluffy. I usually do 2 eggs per person. Pour the eggs into a buttered frying pan.

When the omelet is almost ready, put the steamed broccoli on 1/2 of the eggs and sprinkle small chunks of feta cheese and ground pepper over them. Fold the other half of the egg over and cook until done.

Because the feta cheese is salty, you might want to taste the omelet

Annie Dillard

Pilgrim at Tinkers Creek, *Annie Dillard's first book of prose, won a Pulitzer Prize and has been compared to Thoreau's* Walden. *She has been published in* Atlantic Monthly, Harpers, Poetry, Antaeus, *as well as other magazines and periodicals, and is the author of numerous books of poetry and non-fiction and, more recently, a novel,* The Living.

Aromatic Beef from Java
(very lean)

Fry 1/4 cup sliced onion in a small amount of oil. Add 1 pound well trimmed cubes of chuck, 2 tsp. minced ginger root, a generous sprinkling of nutmeg over all, a generous sprinkling of cloves over all, salt and pepper. Stir—but you don't have to brown it.
Add 1 cup water, 2 Tbsp. soy, 2 Tbsp. plus 1 tsp. sugar, 1 tsp. vinegar. Cover and simmer about an hour. Watch to see if it needs water. Garnish with cilantro.
This has the flavor of the old spices—nutmeg and cloves. It often turns black. It doesn't affect the flavor, which is very good. It's great for a crowd—you don't have to brown it, it reheats, people like it. (Serve with white rice.)

My other standby, on which I'm beginning to live year round (though at first I made it just for company).

Gingered Fruit Glaze

Bring 1/3 cup sugar to boil in 1/3 cup water with a cinnamon stick and 3 slices ginger root. Boil gently 15 minutes. Strain into a glass serving bowl and chill.
Any time after it's chilled, slice fruit into it and stir it up. The glaze is completely transparent—of course it prevents the fruit (except for bananas) from darkening.

I was going to give you my favorite couscous, but it requires fenugreek, which is hard to find. I asked my brother-in-law to get me some, and he said, "I'll just run down to Fenugreek-R-Us."

Carole Nelson Douglas

Formerly an award-winning reporter and feature writer for the St. Paul Pioneer Press *and* St. Paul Dispatch *in Minnesota, Carole Nelson Douglas writes fantasy, historical and contemporary fiction as well as mysteries. Her books include* Cat on a Blue Monday *and* Irene's Last Waltz.

Here is a sinfully tasty treat that begins with split ladyfingers, abuses dessert mixes, and ends with knifework.

Chilled Marble Cheesecake

12 ladyfingers, split
1 envelope unflavored gelatin
1/4 cup cold water
3 8-oz. pkg. cream cheese, softened
1 4-oz. pkg. chocolate-flavor whipped dessert mix
1 3-1/2-oz. pkg. vanilla-flavored whipped dessert mix
1 cup sugar
1/4 tsp. almond extract
1 tsp. grated lemon rind

Line sides of 9-inch springform pan with waxed paper, then ladyfingers (rounded side out). Set aside. Soften gelatin in cold water; dissolve over hot water. Place 1-1/2 pkg. of cream cheese in each of two large bowls. Beat until smooth. Blend 1/2 cup sugar and 2 Tbsp. dissolved gelatin into each bowl; set aside. Prepare chocolate and vanilla desserts separately, as directed. Blend chocolate dessert and almond extract into one bowl of cheese mixture; blend vanilla dessert and lemon rind into remaining bowl of cheese mixture. Drop the mixtures alternately into the prepared pan to give a marbled effect. Using a knife, lightly score top. Chill 6 hours or more. Serves 8 hungry ghouls.

David Drake

Once the Assistant Town Attorney for Chapel Hill, North Carolina, David Drake is now a fulltime writer of science fiction and fantasy. He has published more than 50 stories in magazines and is assistant editor of Whispers. *His books include* The Voyage *and* Tyrannosaur.

Pig Pickin'

Absolutely the only cooking I do is a pig picking in late September for my birthday. I've got a simple iron grate on six post legs. I lean sheet metal around the sides to close it—aluminum roofing for the long sides. This isn't fancy. Another sheet of metal, cardboard, or even a tarp lies over the pig.

The pig is just that a whole—about 100-pound—hog, split up the middle. Unless you've got a larger cooler than mine to transport it and store it the night before, you'll probably have the head removed and maybe the trotters as well.

I get up about six in the morning and build a fire in an open-topped 55-gallon drum with a shovel hole cut in the bottom. There's holes punched about 18" up so that three iron pipes can be thrust through. They hold the larger logs to burn out of the way of the shovel with which you remove coals.

Start with the pig flesh-side down on the grate. Shake the barrel and jab the shovel down into it to knock off coals. Shovel them under the pig on the grate. (Don't build a fire directly under the pig.)

You can do the whole job with hardwood, but it'll take a lot of wood. I've come to the system of keeping a hardwood fire going, but dumping part-bags of charcoal into the bottom of the barrel to pre-heat and ignite. (If you put cold charcoal under the pig, it'll cool the system down before it ignites.)

I have the barrel and grate on a gravel drive. Don't have the barrel too close to the eaves of your house, and it's a good idea to have a charged hose handy while the process continues. Also, don't wear anything you mind getting spark-holes burned into. That includes your own bare skin.

Flip the pig skin-side down about noon. This takes two people and a certain amount of swearing. Baste heavily with barbeque sauce. A friend, writer Karl Wagner, traditionally makes mine. It's different each year but always very hot. The base is vinegar, red pepper, and jalapenos, but there are exotics at whim. Last year's which was wonderful, included Indian Lime Pickle.

The tenderloin should be ready to eat when you flip the pig. When it's my pig, the cook and early guests whittle it out with their pocket knives. I can't tell you how good it tastes.

Depending on variables like the weather, the pig may be ready to carve anywhere from 4-8 p.m. Rain will cool the air and the top sheet, greatly slowing the process.

When the pig's done, slide it onto a carving table of some sort and cut it onto platters. Removing a well-cooked pig is tricky, because it'll tend to stick to the grate and fall apart as you pull. A couple shovels and several helpers are useful. Also friends who don't complain when half the pig falls onto the gravel.

Have pitchers of sauce available for those who want more. If it's been a cool day, you may want to put the hams back on the fire for a time.

It's not really tricky, though I've learned a lot of refinements over the 20-odd years I've been doing this. Most of them are a matter of location, available materials, and taste.

Clyde Edgerton

Clyde Edgerton's first novel, Raney, *evoked comparisons to Mark Twain and James Thurber. He has taught English and writing at several colleges, most recently Duke University. Among his other novels are* Walking Across Egypt *and* In Memory of Junior.

Mattie Rigsbee of *Walking Across Egypt* sends this recipe.

Cornbread

1) Mix 2 or 3 cups of sifted corn meal (white or yellow) with warm water until it is mushy. Add salt. Mix again.
2) Heat vegetable oil (high heat) in frying pan—oil should be about 1/4 to 1/2 inch deep. When oil is hot, drop small patties of corn meal mush into oil, pressing each flat with a fork.
3) Turn heat to medium.
4) When cornbread is brown on one side, turn it over.
5) When cornbread is brown on both sides, drain on paper towel.
6) Eat.

                      Sincerely,
                      Mattie Rigsbee

Candace Flynt

A former reporter and feature writer, Candace Flynt is the author of three acclaimed novels, Chasing Dad, Sins of Omission *and* Mother Love. *Her stories have appeared in* Greensboro Review, Carolina Quarterly, Redbook, *and* Atlanta Monthly. *She lives in Greensboro, North Carolina.*

None of my female characters can cook, although the males frequently can. Regularly, though, one of my female characters is called upon to perform in the kitchen. The only thing she knows to do is pull out a fail-safe recipe, such as the one that follows. "Katherine's" Beef Tenderloin, as I can attest, cannot be messed up. Despite the recipe's simplicity, both my characters and I still have to reread it every time.

"Katherine's" Beef Tenderloin

1 high quality beef tenderloin
3 cloves garlic
Salt and pepper

Preheat oven to 425 degrees. Sliver garlic and insert in numerous 1/2" slits in beef. Generously salt and pepper. Cook for 10 minutes at 425 degrees. Reduce heat to 350 degrees. For rare meat, continue cooking for 25 minutes. For medium rare meat, continue cooking for 40 minutes. Cool a minimum of 10 minutes before serving.

My first writing job was as a reporter for the Greensboro *News & Record* in 1969 when I was just out of college. The pay was a scant $100 a week. After taxes and insurance I took home somewhere between $85 and $87. I didn't have much money for food, certainly not the kind of food that's easy to cook because it's so fine to begin with—the aforementioned beef tenderloin, for example. I instead ate things like tuna and hot dog casseroles. If you happen to be living in a garret, such dishes are good on the budget. Also, if you have no cooking talent, they're like boiling water.

Later in life, when I could afford to buy a beef tenderloin for guests, I had a dinner party with long time friends who by that time had grown used to nice meals at my house. This particular evening, though, I'd kept the menu a secret. Guess what I served? The joke turned out to be—more or less—on me. No one believed I didn't have a "real" meal hidden in the kitchen...until they went in and looked.

Hot Dog Casserole for Two

4 or 5 hot dogs cut in chunks
3 or 4 potatoes peeled and cut up
1 coarsely chopped onion
4 slices of bacon
1/2 cup of grated cheddar cheese

The amount of each ingredient can be varied according to level of hunger. Bacon and/or cheese may be omitted. Combine hot dogs, potatoes, onions, and bacon in buttered casserole dish. Cover and bake at 350 degrees for 1 hour. Uncover and sprinkle cheese on top.

Alan Dean Foster

The author of numerous short stories, novels and film novelizations, Alan Dean Foster has taught screeenwriting, literature and film history at UCLA and Los Angeles City College. His books include The Star Trek Logs *and* The Spoils of War.

    Here's a real recipe. The difficulty's not in the cooking but in the shopping....

    To catch piranha, find a small, still-water side stream off the main river and anchor near its mouth (do not tie up to a tree or the ants will getcha). Bait hook with any available meat and place pole in water.

Wait five to 10 seconds.

When piranha bites, jerk pole sharply to set hook, then flip line over shoulder and snap pole sharply back forward, thus neatly dislodging hook and leaving piranha in bottom of boat. Keep feet up on seats whenever possible and wear heavy boots at all times, as piranha will snap at anything within reach for 10 to 30 minutes.

Pan-Fried Garlic Piranha

Dust Piranha fillets with lemon pepper and a pinch of salt, then place in lightly oiled pan. Turn fillets, then roll in pan containing flour and breadcrumbs. Set aside. Slice 1 clove of fresh garlic per piranha and place aside.

After fillets are suitably crumbed, place butter to size in cast-iron skillet and heat on open fire until skillet is glazed and sizzling. Add sliced garlic and fillets. Turn both garlic and fillets until nicely browned. Add capers and serve. Piranha have many small bones and taste like trout.

Marianne Gingher

Marianne Gingher's first novel, Bobby Rex's Greatest Hit, *received the Sir Walter Raleigh Award and was named by the American Library Association as one of the Best Books for Young Adults for 1986. It was made into a television movie in 1993,* Just My Imagination, *starring Jean Smart and Tom Wopat. She also is the author an a short story collection,* Teen Angel, *and teaches English at the University of North Carolina at Chapel Hill.*

Here's a recipe for what I will call "Sweetheart Cherry Pie." This is the recipe my heroine in *Bobby Rex's Greatest Hit*, Pally Thompson, used to bake the cherry pie that she took over to Billy Pickup. After one bite of that pie, Billy was smitten for life, and Bobby Rex Moseley was history to Pally's heart. A lot of sacrifice and sweat goes into this pie. You have to want to love somebody to make it turn out the best. You also have to believe in magic and hold your breath and pray a lot that the pie will turn out as you make it. It ought to be a steaming hot day in mid-summer when you set to work in your kitchen pre-heating the oven. You ought not to have air-conditioning. If you know some old rock and roll tunes from the fifties, sing them while you roll out your pastry. If your pie turns out the way Pally's did, somebody who eats it will fall in love with you big-time. Happily married women should avoid this recipe, unless they're cooking exclusively for their husbands.

Sweetheart Cherry Pie

Pastry:
2 cups all purpose flour
2/3 cup shortening
Several Tbsp. cold water
Dash of salt

Mix flour and shortening in a bowl until crumbly looking. Add salt. Add about 4-6 Tbsp. of ice-cold water. Depending on the humidity the pastry will be too dry if not enough water is added. But you don't want the pastry to be gooey. Stir until mixture forms a ball. Consistency is a little bit drier than Play-Doh. Divide ball in half. Roll out first half and put in round glass pie plate. Sprinkle with a tablespoon of cinnamon mixed with sugar in equal parts. Fill with the following:

Filling:
1 can tart red pitted cherries. DO NOT buy cherry filling
1 cup BROWN sugar
2 Tbsp. butter
3 Tbsp. flour
1 tsp. vanilla or almond extract
1/2 tsp. pure ground cinnamon

Nikki Giovanni

*Nikki Giovanni writes poetry for children and is also a recording artist, performer, and lecturer. Among her books are E*go-Tripping & Other Poems for Young People *and* Sacred Cows...and Other Edibles.

As a working mother, writer, main support of two dogs, with a father who had had a stroke, I early on discovered the convenience of the Clay Cooker. I think some Mayan mother who was sick of the kids messing up the house took their clay and threw it into the fire. When she noticed it had been properly fired instead of becoming ashes she, in the infinite curiosity of the female, placed something in it, probably some small fowl just to see what would happen. When it came out delicious a wonderful work saver had been discovered.

I believe in the Clay Cooker. My life would be different, markedly so, without it. It sends wonderful smells throughout the day and is hot when you are ready for it. My recipe is for a Clay Cooker.

Frozen Lamb Shank in Clay Cooker

Needed:
Clay Cooker, parchment paper, white wine, lamb shank, celery, onions, carrots, some kind of garlic, curry, fennel.
Soak the cooker top and bottom with cold water for 20 minutes. Pull off a part of the parchment paper and line the pot. I usually start with frozen meat.
Rinse the shank and place in the pot.
Cut up 3 or 4 carrots which have been peeled.

Cut up 2 or 3 celery stalks which have been made free of strings. You can leave the leaves of the stalks since they add flavor.
Quarter 2 medium sized onions.
Generously sprinkle garlic salt or minced garlic.
Generously add fennel,
A good pinch of curry should be added,
Use about 1/4 cup of white, not red, wine. If shank is large use 1/2 cup,
Cover and place in cold oven,
Start oven at 250 for 3-4 hours (use your timer to start it late if you want dinner at 7 pm),
Note: Do not add regular salt to this,
I usually cook couscous or polenta if I have time. Rice is good also, and a green salad.

James M. Goode

James M. Goode's first book, The Outdoor Sculpture of Washington, D.C. *was the result of research he did for walking tours he conducted for Smithsonian Resident Associates. His book* Best Addresses, *a survey of Washington's grand old apartment houses, grew out of his fascination with architectural history.*

My Mother's Bread Pudding

2 eggs
1/4 lb. butter, melted
1 cup sugar
1 cup sweet milk
2-1/2 cups crumbled cold biscuits
1 tsp. vanilla or cinnamon

Use leftover homemade biscuits. Mix all ingredients well, and pour into a round buttered baking dish. Cover the whole with a thick coating of brown sugar and dots of butter. Bake at 350 degrees about 30 minutes to a golden brown.
Optional: Serve warm with lemon sauce or scoop of ice cream.

Sue Grafton

A scriptwriter for television movies before beginning her best-selling alphabetical series of mysteries starring Kinsey Milhone, private eye, Sue Grafton is president of the Mystery Writers of America. Her novel The Lolly-Madonna War *was made into a movie for which she wrote the screenplay. She also co-wrote the pilot for the TV series* Seven Brides for Seven Brothers.

Kinsey admitted to me in private that she's been a little put out about the fact that Robert Parker's Spenser has an entire cookbook devoted to his recipes while she has none. Though I've never spelled it out in excrutiating detail (until now), I am revealing the secret family recipe for the Kinsey Millhone Peanut-Butter-and-Pickle Sandwich.

The Kinsey Millhone Famous Peanut Butter & Pickle Sandwich

2 slices of Health-Nut Bread, or some whole grain
Gobs of Jif Crunchy Peanut Butter (no substitutions, please)
Vlasik Sweet Butter Chips (again, no substitutions or we can't be responsible for the results)*

Spread gobs of Jif Crunch Peanut Butter on 1 slice of Health-Nut bread. Place 6 or 7 Vlasik Sweet Butter Chips on the peanut butter. Top with second slice of bread. Cut on the diagonal. Serves 1.

*When we mentioned Vlasik Sweet Butter Chips by name in a

well-known food-related magazine, Vlasik sent us a case of sweet butter chips. Let's hope the Jif Crunchy Peanut Butter people are just as generous in response to our product loyalty.

Linda Grant

The president of Sisters in Crime, Linda Grant a former teacher of high school English and Peace Corps volunteer, is the author of a series of novels featuring a female private investigator in San Francisco. Two, *Random Access Murder* and *Love Nor Money* were nominated for Anthony awards.

A private investigator doesn't have a lot of time for cooking what with rooting out evil and smacking around bad guys. Catherine Sayler, the protagonist of my mystery series would rather face an armed assailant than a recipe with more than six ingredients. To see that she doesn't starve to death, I've provided her with what every woman needs—a sexy lover who can cook. And since this lover is an unreformed sixties person, many of his meals are vegetarian. One of his favorite recipes (and mine) comes from Mollie Katzen's *Moosewood Cookbook*. It features every hippie's favorite vegetable, easy to grow and prolific as hell: zucchini. This one's a real winner, even with Catherine's 14-year-old niece who considers vegetables an alien life form.

Zucchini-Feta Pancakes

    4 eggs, separated (yolks optional)
    4 packed cups coarsely grated zucchini (about 4 7-inchers)
    1 cup finely crumbled feta cheese
    1/2 cup finely minced scallions
    1 tsp. dried mint (or 1 Tbsp. fresh, finely minced)

A little salt (optional, to taste)
Lots of black pepper
1/3 cup flour
Oil for frying
Sour cream or yogurt for topping

Beat the egg white until stiff. In a medium-size bowl, combine zucchini, egg yolks (or not), feta, scallions, seasonings, and flour. Mix well. Fold the egg whites into the zucchini mixture. Heat a little oil in a heavy skillet. When it is very hot, add spoonfuls of batter, and fry on both sides until golden and crisp. Serve immediately, topped with sour cream or yogurt. Serves about 4. Preparation time: 30 minutes.

Daniel Halpern

Formerly editor of American Poetry Anthology, *Daniel Halpern is editor-in-chief of Ecco Press. An instructor of poetry and fiction workshops, he has received Robert Frost and NEA Fellowships as well as winning the Jessie Rehder Poetry Award. His books include* Our Private Lives *and* Foreign Neon: Poems.

This is one of my favorite warm weather pastas—quick, intense, unusual.

Ruote* With Corn, Scallions and Coriander

1 lb. ruote, or fusilli
2 Tbsp. lime juice
2 Tbsp. rice vinegar
1/2 cup olive oil
Salt and freshly ground pepper to taste
2 cups cooked fresh corn kernels (3 cobs), or 2 10-oz. pkg. frozen corn
6 scallions with their greens, chopped finely
1/4 cup packed chopped fresh coriander

Cook the pasta until al dente, drain well, and place it in a large bowl.
In a small bowl, whisk together the lime juice, rice vinegar, olive oil, and pepper and salt and toss it with the pasta.
Add the corn, scallions, and coriander and toss well. Allow the pasta to sit at room temperature for an hour or so before serving.
Serves 6-8
*Cartwheel-shaped pasta

Cynthia Harrod-Eagles

Born in London, Cynthia Harrod-Eagles studied at the University of Edinburgh and University College, London. Noted for her historical novels, she also has written three mysteries featuring Inspector Bill Slider, which have been published in this country.

I offer you Bill Slider's recipe for spaghetti bolognese. Bill, hero of *Orchestrated Death, Death Watch, Death to Go*, and many more adventures yet to be committed to print, enjoys his food very much and is fond of cooking, as long as it isn't too finicking. He writes:

"As far as I know, nothing has yet been written on the importance of spaghetti bolognese in smoothing the course of true love. My partner, Detective Sergeant Jim Atherton, woos his ladies with terrine of three mushrooms and noisettes of lamb with gooseberry coulis; I am a strictly one-pot man, and in my experience there is no happier dish to prepare and eat with the person of your choice than a really rich and powerful bolognese sauce, served over al dente spaghetti, and accompanied by lots of homemade garlic bread and a bottle of chianti. Love bubbles in every aromatic spoonful, and by the time you're scraping the pot together for the crusty bit at the bottom, she is yours forever. This is a binding ceremony, so don't cook spaghetti bolognese with someone you don't want to spend the rest of your life with!

Spaghetti Bolognese

1 large onion
2-3 large cloves garlic
8 oz. ground beef

4 oz. chicken livers
2 rashers (slices) smoked streaky bacon (or 2 oz smoked ham)
1 14 oz. tin plum tomatoes
2-3 Tbsp. tomato paste
1 glass red wine
2 stock cubes
Dried basil, oregano and tarragon
Olive oil
Black pepper

Put on a large pan of salted water to heat for the spaghetti while you make the sauce. Weigh out the spaghetti—3 oz. per person or 4 oz. if you are really hungry. This recipe will make enough sauce for 4 greedy or 6 restrained people.

For the sauce, heat a little olive oil in a saucepan. Chop the onion, garlic and bacon and fry gently until the onion softens. Chop the chicken livers (not too small) and brown them. Add the ground beef and brown it while mixing it with the onion, etc., in the pan. Crumble the stock cubes over, add the wine and mix in. Now add the tomatoes, breaking them up with a knife and mixing them in. Add the tomato paste, oregano and basil to taste (you will learn how much herb you like in your sauce; if you haven't done it before, try half a tablespoon of each to begin with) and plenty of freshly-ground black pepper. Turn the heat down to a gentle simmer, partly cover the pot, and cook for 8-10 minutes. (If the sauce looks too liquid after this, remove the lid completely and let it reduce for 5 minutes or so until it is the consistency you like. As long as you cook it gently, you won't overcook it.)

By this time the water should be boiling for the spaghetti. Cook it for 8 to 10 minutes according to taste.

While it is cooking, stir the sauce from time to time, and with about 3 minutes to go add the tarragon (it loses its taste if cooked too long).

When the spaghetti is done, the sauce should be ready too (this is such a quick and easy meal!) Serve with grated Parmesan cheese, if liked, garlic bread and a dry Italian wine—Chianti, Valpolicella or Montepulciano are the best if you can get them.

Carolyn Hart

Carolyn Hart is the author of eight mysteries featuring Annie Darling, including Something Wicked, *which won both an Agatha and an Anthony Award;* Honeymoon with Murder, *which won an Anthony; and* A Little Class on Murder *which won a Macavity Award. She lives in Oklahoma City.*

    In my Death on Demand mysteries, Annie Laurance (later Darling) never cooks.
    Guess why?
    I never cook.
    That doesn't mean that I (and Annie) don't like food.
    It means I was always a mediocre cook.
    I tried.
    But if I did a recipe, it came out tasting—well—tasteless. My mother, my mother-in-law, my sister-in-law, my daughter have simply to walk into a kitchen and miraculous—to me—events occur, resulting in delicious, scrumptious, delectable dishes.
    But with age comes cunning.
    Even I can sometimes create (sort of, let's not quibble) something yummy.
    To wit: the famous raspberry brownies celebrated in the Death on Demand mysteries and beloved of Annie.
    And it's EASY.

Raspberry Brownies

    Buy a Betty Crocker brownie mix, follow the directions. Then

take about 4 Tbsp. of raspberry jam (you know that fancy cooks are always a bit loose about amounts) and swirl the jam through the mixture. Bake as directed.
Voila, raspberry brownies!

Okay, so it isn't Cordon Bleu. It isn't original. But it IS good.

Anthony Hecht

Anthony Hecht has won the Pulitzer Prize for poetry as well as the Prix de Rome, Miles Poetry Prize and the Russell Loines Award. He's also received Guggenheim and Ford Foundation Fellowships as well as one from the Academy of American Poets. He has taught at many colleges and unversities. His books include The Hidden Law: The Poetry of W.H. Auden, *and* Transparent Man.

I've had the great good fortune to have married a superb cook, the author of four cookbooks, who writes under her own name of Helen Hecht, and whose works include *Simple Pleasures*, *Cold Cuisine*, and *Cuisine for All Seasons*. So for many years I have retired entirely from the kitchen range and have allowed myself to be spoiled and pampered.

In my old bachelor days I used to make a few show-off meals (a lamb curry with lots of condiments on the side; a hearty stew of kidneys and lentils; a cold squid salad) to impress a few friends, but I was content to defrost a solitary meal when home alone. I am therefore not au courant as a cook. But I am pleased to say that one old recipe I picked up from an Armenian friend pleased my wife enough for her to appropriate it in her book called *Cold Cuisine*, a book devoted to food that can be served cold in summertime. One of the great virtues of this recipe, however, which we have taken to calling "Byzantine Artichokes," is that it can be served either hot or cold.

Byzantine Artichokes

6 large artichokes
2 medium onions, sliced
1 Tbsp. sugar
Juice of two lemons
2/3 cup of olive or peanut oil
1 cup water
Salt & pepper
Red pepper flakes (optional)

Remove stems from bottoms of artichokes so that they can sit flat in a cooking pot. Also cut off tops of artichokes at mid-point, discarding tops. Put the bottoms into a cookpot, so that they sit flat and side by side. Add all ingredients, and, if desired, some red pepper flakes. Cook covered tightly without opening the lid over medium heat for 1 hour. This can serve as a vegetable course for 6, a light meal for 6, or after cooling, a salad course for 6. It is precisely this versatility that recommended the dish to a bachelor.

Joan Hess

A founder of Sisters in Crime, mystery writer Joan Hess is author of the Claire Malloy series and the popular Maggody books. She is a winner of the American Mystery Award and an Agatha. Her newest book is Martians in Maggody.

[From Best-Loved Recipes from Ruby Bee's Bar & Grill, Maggody Arkansas]

Dear Neighbors,

A lot of you have been pestering me something awful to write up a few of my favorite recipes, so I did. I suppose I'll donate the profits to the Missionary Society, even if smarmy Mrs. Jim Bob is the president and forever carryin' on about how high and mighty she is.

If you fret about cholesterol and calories, you're plum out of luck. The only person in Maggody who might need to worry about her weight (yes, Dahlia, I mean you), can't be bothered, which is why she topped three hundred pounds last year.

        Yours truly,
        Ruby Bee

Festive Green Bean Casserole

2 cans french-cut green beans, drained
1 can cream of mushroom soup
1 can onion rings
3 Tbsp. chopped pimentos

Open the cans, mix everything up real good, saving some of the onion rings to sprinkle on the top for decoration. Bake it at 350 degrees until it's bubbly. It doesn't take very long.

It has been brought to my attention that Elsie McMay has been telling everyone who'll listen that you ought to add a can of sliced water chestnuts to make it crunch. Estelle went so far as to say she prefers it that way, but she ain't got the sense God gave a goose when it comes to the finer things in life.

If you want to ruin a perfectly good recipe by adding water chestnuts, it's none of my business. All I can say is that lady lawyer in *Much Ado About Maggody* flat out told me that she didn't like water chestnuts. I'm not sure if she said it before or after the bank burned up and the body was found. Johnna Mae Nookim was tickled pink—up until they arrested her. It's a darn good thing Estelle and I figured she was innocent.

Chicken Fried Steak With Cream Gravy

4 pieces of round steak, about 5 ounces each
1 cup flour
Salt and pepper
1 egg, lightly beaten
1-1/2 cups milk
1/4 cup bacon drippings

First you pound the meat with one of those fancy mallets, or with the edge of a saucer, which has worked just fine for me for some 40 odd years.

Put some salt and pepper in flour, then dredge each piece of meat in it. Mix 1/2 cup milk with the egg. Dunk the meat in this, and back again in the flour.

Using a heavy black skillet, pan fry 'em in the drippings until they're nice and brown, drain on a paper towel, and pop 'em in a warm oven.

Drain off all but 2 Tbs. of the drippings. Stir in 2 Tbs. of the flour, scrape the bottom of the pan real good, and pour in 1 cup of milk. Continue stirring over medium heat until the gravy gets thick. Add

more milk if it gets too thick, and taste it to see if it needs more salt and pepper.
Serves Hammet Buchanon or 4 regular folks.

Estelle Oppers's Fancy Snowflake Salad

1 pkg. cherry gelatin
1 pkg. raspberry gelatin
1 can white seedless cherries
1 cup chopped pecans
1 large can crushed pineapple
2 cans cold Coca Cola
1 3-oz. pkg. of cream cheese, frozen

Drain the cherries and pineapple into a saucepan and heat the juices until they're steamy. Dissolve the gelatins in this, then add the fruit and nuts.
Pour in both cans of Coca Cola. Dump the mixture in a pretty mold, and chill until it's set.
Dip the mold in warm water until the salad is loose enough to slip onto a platter. Then get out the frozen cream cheese and grate it so it looks like snow. If this ain't fancy, I don't know what is.
—E.O.

I made this for those Hollywood actors when they were in town to shoot the X-rated movie. Famous Miss Kitty Kaye just loved it, and I was fixing another batch special her for when she got herself killed. That was in Mortal Remains in Maggody, I seem to recall.
—R. B. H.

Beans 'n Ham

4 cups pinto beans
1 cup chopped ham
1/2 tsp. cayenne pepper
1 Tbsp. Worchestershire sauce
1/4 tsp. black pepper

1 tsp. red pepper sauce
1 Tbsp. baking soda*
1 large onion, chopped up
1/8 to 1 tsp. garlic powder

Soak the beans in water with the baking soda for an hour. Drain off the water and rinse the beans.

Then add everything and enough water to cover 'em, and start simmering on low heat and adding more water when you see fit to. This may take anywheres from 3 1/2 to 5 hours, dependin' on how mushy you like your beans.

Even Arly could fix these and catch herself a man instead of sulking in her apartment. She's still a might grumpy about that nice young fellow I fixed her up with in the tale I call Mischief in Maggody. How was I supposed to know he was up to no good? Madam Celeste was the town's new mind-reader, not me.

*The baking soda's supposed to take care of a certain problem that comes with eatin' beans (although there ain't nothing gonna stop Raz Buchanon from making his presence remembered for a long while).

Arly's Favorite Peach Cobbler

8 peaches, peeled and sliced
2/3 cup sugar
Cinnamon to taste

You need big, plump, juicy peaches, so I guess if you live in Noow Yark City, you got yourself a humdinger of a problem. Anyway, spread the sliced peaches in a buttered pan. Sprinkle the sugar and some cinnamon on 'em.

1 egg beaten
1/3 cup milk
3 Tbsp. melted Crisco

1/4 cup sugar
2 tsp. baking powder
1/2 tsp. salt
1 cup flour

Mix all of the above together real good and pour it over the peaches. Bake at 375 degrees for 30 minutes or so.

Vanilla ice cream goes good on the cobbler. When I served it that way to the ornery EPA bureaucrat that Mayor Jim Bob kidnapped and locked up in the Flamingo Motel in *Malice in Maggody*, I thought he'd cry...like he did when he met slutty Robin Buchanon. Lordy, she was as mean as her hide would hold, and then some. Her sassy bushcolts weren't no better.

Tony Hillerman

A past president of the Mystery Writers of America, Tony Hillerman has received their Edgar and Grand Master Awards. Among his other honors are the Center for the American Indian's Ambassador Award, the Silver Spur Award for best novel set in the West, and the Navajo Tribe's Special Friend Award. His many bestselling novels include Coyote Waits, Talking God, A Thief of Time *and* Dance Hall of the Dead.

The recipe for Navajo Tacos, as practiced out in the Navajo Mountain territory, is approximately as follows:

Navajo Tacos

Several pounds of chopped up mutton (or goat, if mutton is unavailable).
Stew same until relatively tender in iron pot over propane burner (or woodfire if propane supply exhausted).
Mix in large quantities of ground red chili. (Note: on the Big Reservation and in the world of civilized dining the word "chili" means the fruit of the chili plant as grown around Hatch, New Mexico, if you like it hot, or around mountain valleys around Chimayo if you like it milder. It is no relation to what passes for chili in Texas, which seems to be a mixture of tomato sauce, pepper, cumin and pink paint.)
Prepare bread dough, roll out into sheets about 8 millimeters thick with the diameter of a medium Pizza Hut pizza.

Drop bread discs into iron pot in which mutton grease is at a bubbling boil. (Grease left over from last year seems to be preferred.)

When bread attains a bubbled-up brown crust, fish out of grease, place on plate, pour on thick layer of stewed mutton and chili. Cover this with light coating of chopped onions mixed with chopped and pre-boiled green chili and whatever other edible herbs are in season and available.

Serve steaming hot, and with glass of cold orange soda pop on the left side of the plate and glass of Alka-Seltzer on the right.

Ann Hood

Ann Hood's most recent novel Places to Spend the Night *was a Literary Guild selection. Her short stories and essays have appeared in many publications including* Mademoiselle, Redbook, Seventeen, Self *and others. She has been on the staff of Breadloaf Writers' Workshop and taught creative writing at Columbia University.*

In my novel, *Something Blue,* Jasper believes there is a food to cure everything. Turkey, he says, cures jet lag. I must admit that he borrowed that philosphy from me! Here is my recipe to cure a broken heart. It is decadent, fattening and garlicky!

Spaghetti Carbonara

12 oz. fresh spaghetti
2 Tbsp. olive oil
1 lb. bacon or pancetta, chopped
4 cloves of minced garlic
1 Tbsp. oregano
Lots of freshly ground black pepper
3 eggs, beaten
lots of freshly grated Parmesan cheese (NOT the stuff in those green cans off the shelf)

Heat olive oil in large skillet. Add bacon, garlic and oregano. Cook over slow heat until bacon is crispy and brown. While bacon cooks, make spaghetti according to pkg. directions. Drain. Toss with beaten eggs. When well mixed add UNDRAINED bacon.

Toss. Add lots and lots of parmesan, tossing until spaghetti is well coated. If extremely heartbroken, serve with even more parmesan on top.

Belinda Hurmence

Belinda Hurmence's books for children and young adults have received the Parent's Choice Award, American Library Association Notable Book Award and many others. Formerly an editor at Mademoiselle, *she also was executive editor of* Flair Magazine. *Among her books are* The Nightwalker *and* A Girl Called Boy.

Lifetime Hot Sauce

1 lb. jalapeno peppers
1 lb. green tomatoes
1 cup white vinegar
1 Tbsp. sea salt
1 tsp. ground turmeric

Slice off pepper stems and quarter the tomatoes. Grind together, or blend or process the vegetables. (Wear rubber gloves and safety glasses—no kidding). Add vinegar and seasonings. Bring all ingredients to a boil over medium heat. Seal in hot half-pint jelly jars. Yield: 6 plus jars.

Note: This sauce probably needs a new name; Lifetime was what my family called it originally before I adulterated the ingredients with tomato. In recent years I added the tomato in response to widespread blisters, also demand. The recipe makes a lot for sissies—i.e., for those not reared on Tex-Mex, as I was. Give five jars of your yield away and keep the one plus for your own "enjoyment."

Try using a teaspoonful in egg salad, grilled cheese sandwiches, bean dip, roast chicken, peanut butter, omelets, and in more conventional sauces, such as tartar, barbecue, hollandaise and remoulade.

Faye Kellerman

The author of seven novels including the acclaimed historical mystery The Quality of Mercy, *and* False Prophet, *Faye Kellerman, lives with her husband, Jonathan Kellerman, also a novelist, and their four children.*

[A postscript to *False Prophet*.]

We leave Peter and Rina as they anxiously await the arrival of their first child together. It is a rather disconcerting place to stop for those who are curious about the baby. Not to fret: the new family will be revealed in the next novel in the series from Morrow entitled *Grievous Sin*. Having given birth to four children, I am no stranger to the state of pregnancy. Nor was I, like Rina, immune from pregnancy cravings. Although Rina and I keep the dietary laws of traditional Judaism, we still have room for creativity in the kitchen. Living in Los Angeles, we're influenced by regional cuisine as exemplified by Rina's southwestern meal in *False Prophet*. Here is her personal recipe for Salsa Chicken. She might serve this entree with wild rice and a fresh avocado-and-grapefruit salad. Enjoy!

Salsa Chicken

4 large tomatoes, coarsely chopped
1 small onion, finely chopped
1 small green pepper, seeded and diced
1 clove fresh minced garlic
2 Tbsp. fresh lemon juice
2 Tbsp. minced fresh coriander

2 tsp. minced fresh parsley
1/2 tsp. salt
1/2 tsp. pepper
2 Tbsp. flour
1/2 tsp. garlic powder
1/2 tsp. salt
1/2 tsp. pepper
6 boneless chicken breasts (each 1/2 " thick)
Oil for frying
Parsley sprigs and lemon slices for garnish

In a medium bowl, mix together the tomatoes, onion, green pepper, garlic, lemon juice, coriander, parsley, salt, and pepper. Set aside in refrigerator for at least 2 hours.
Preheat oven to 350 degrees.
In a separate bowl, mix together the flour, garlic powder, salt, and pepper. Dredge the chicken in the dry mixture, then saute in oil until the chicken turns slightly brown. Place the chicken in a shallow, greased baking pan and bake for 30 minutes or until done to taste. Remove the chicken from the oven and place on a serving platter. Decorate with parsley sprigs and lemon slices. Serve hot with salsa on the side. Serves 6.

Jonathan Kellerman

After a distinguished career in child psychology, Jonathan Kellerman turned to writing fiction full-time, producing his popular series of Alex Delaware novels. More than 13 million copies of his books are now in print. Among them are Devil's Waltz, Bad Love *and* The Butcher's Theater.

I've exhausted my culinary expertise in two other cookbooks. Suffice it to say that Alex Delaware's cholesterol is low and he enjoys a good steak, now and then. Try a rib steak, marinated in soy sauce, red wine, black pepper, garlic, cooked medium rare leaning toward rare. Some kind of green salad with a light vinaigrette, some fettucine with basil, olive oil and garlic. Give the dog some, too. He/she does not live by kibble alone. Very cold passion fruit iced tea or more wine if you're so inclined. Espresso or Turkish coffee. Fresh watermelon. Goodnight.

Stephen King

Many of Stephen King's immensely popular novels have been made into movies, among them The Shining, Cujo *and* The Stand. *He lives in central Maine with his wife Tabitha, also a writer.*

My kids love this. I only make it when my wife, Tabby, isn't home. She won't eat it, in fact doesn't even like to look at it.

Lunchtime Gloop

2 cans Franco American Spaghetti (without meat balls)
1 lb. cheap, greasy hamburger

Brown hamburg in large skillet. Add Franco American Spaghetti and cook till heated through. Do not drain hamburg, or it won't be properly greasy. Burn on pan if you want—that will only improve the flavor. Serve with buttered Wonder Bread.

Christina Baker Kline

A graduate of Yale and Cambridge, Christina Baker Kline was a Henry Hoyns Fellow in writing at the University of Virginia. She now lives in New York City and teaches creative writing at New York University and Yale. Sweet Water *is her first novel.*

I love to cook—many writers do, don't you think? Something about simmering plots and slow-cooking ideas, I guess. At any rate, there's nothing better than a homemade split pea soup bubbling on the stove while you're working on a particularly difficult paragraph. You can always go in and stir it if you need a reason for a break.

This recipe is one that my character Cassie, in *Sweet Water*, would love. In fact, I think it's already a basic part of her very basic cooking repertoire, and here's why: Cassie is a sweet girl—who grew up in a restaurant, so you'd think she'd know better!—but she doesn't have much interest in cooking. In the novel, in fact, we don't see her making anything more complicated than a can of soup. But she does like to have friends over, and she also likes people to think she spent lots of time making a special dinner (who doesn't?). So this recipe is perfect for her. It's quick, easy, elegant, and, best of all, it tastes like it took hours to prepare!

I love to make this pasta dish for dinner parties, with a first course of salad (fresh spinach tossed with a light homemmade vinaigrette, topped with roasted red pepper strips, crumbled goat cheese, and toasted pine nuts), a crusty loaf of bread, and sorbet for dessert.

Chicken and Tarragon in a Creamy Tomato Sauce Over Linguine

1/3 cup butter
3 Tbsp. dry white vermouth
4 boned chicken breast halves, skinned and cubed
1-1/2 Tbsp. whiskey
1/3 cup chicken broth
1-1/3 cup heavy or whipping cream
4 large garlic cloves, chopped
Salt
Lots of freshly ground black pepper
1 medium onion, finely chopped
1/2 cup finely chopped fresh parsley
4 medium ripe tomatoes, plus 3 Tbsp. seeded and chopped for garnish
3 Tbsp. dried tarragon
Grated Parmesan cheese
1 lb. linguine (or spaghettini)

Melt butter in a large skillet. Add chicken and saute until lightly browned, about 5 minutes. Remove chicken to a plate. Add garlic and onion to skillet, and cook until tender, about 3 minutes. Pour in whiskey, vermouth, and chicken broth, and cook on high heat until reduced by about 2/3. Stir in cream, salt, and pepper, and cook on high heat until sauce thickens slightly.

Lower heat and add cooked chicken. Simmer to heat through, about 3 minutes, stir in parsley, and taste for seasoning. Toss with hot pasta in a serving bowl, garnish with parsley, and serve. Pass grated Parmesan cheese and the pepper mill for each person to add to taste. Serves 6.

Rosalind Laker

The author of 18 historical novels including Banners of Silk, To Dance With Kings, *and most recently,* The Sugar Pavilion, *Rosalind Laker lives in Sussex, England.* Orchids and Diamonds, *which is set in France and Italy and the world of "haute couture," will be published in January, 1995.*

In *The Sugar Pavilion* the heroine is a confectioner; therefore a recipe for something sweet. The following dessert is the easiest in the world to make and everybody loves it.

Norwegian Cream

Drain a tin of sweet cooked rice. Beat 1 pt. of dairy cream until fairly stiff. Fold rice into it. Serve with a jug of sieved juice from cooked and sweetened raspberries. It serves 4 people deliciously.

Madeleine L'Engle

Madeleine L'Engle, who writes for children and adults, won the Newbery medal for her popular children's book, A Wrinkle in Time. *She intersperses writing and teaching with raising three children and maintaining an apartment in New York and a farmhouse which is called "Crosswicks" which she has written about in* Crosswicks Journal.

Meg's mother, in *A Wrinkle in Time* and the other Murry family books, often cooks dinner over the Bunsen Burner in her lab, while pondering the world of subatomic particles. This is a good recipe for that kind of cooking.

Pollo Verde

Boned chicken breasts. These can be cooked in the sauce, or if you happen to be near a kitchen, in the oven

The sauce:
A lot of cilantro
4 scallions, greens and all
4 leaves of romaine lettuce (don't ask me why, but they are included in the recipe which is in a friend's cookbook somewhere or other)
1 large sweet onion
Green salsa or hot green tiny tomatoes (to taste)

Chop all these in the food processor if you're in the kitchen. In the lab they can probably be chopped with a scalpel. Simmer. A little white wine can be added if more liquid is needed. At the end add some no-fat yogurt and some lo-fat sour cream. The chicken can be added here if it's been cooked in the oven. Otherwise, cut it in small pieces and cook it with the sauce. Serve over yellow rice.

Charlotte MacLeod

Charlotte MacLeod is known as the Queen of the Whimsical Whodunit for her novels featuring amateur detectives Sarah Kelling and Peter Shandy and other engaging and eccentric characters. Among her books are The Withdrawing Room *and* Something in the Water.

It just so happens that the July, 1994, issue of the CM (Charlotte MacLeod) newsletter carried a recipe for a tea bread that I often make and seldom get to keep for long. I forgot to mention greasing the pan...which is optional on the non-stick ones but, being of a suspicious nature as mystery writers have to be, I usually grease it anyway. Also, I mention an 8"x8" pan, but have since found that a 7"x10" one works even better.

[From the newsletter]

Some readers wish that Charlotte would write more books faster. Others wish she'd break down and reveal her secret formula for what has become known around the MacLeod kitchen as tea bread.

Actually it started out as muffins. Folks in the northeast corner of the map are big on muffins. In fact it's said that no tourist is allowed to leave the area without having eaten at least one and nobody seems to balk at doing so. Charlotte herself has baked so many muffins over the years that she claims she could do it with her eyes shut and the mixing bowl behind her back, though she's never been seen to try.

Part of the fascination with regard to Charlotte's muffins used to be that one never knew what she was going to put into them. At long last, however, she has come up with what seems to be the Ultimate Recipe. She has even revised her modus operandi. This occurred one day when she was scrubbing an aged and battered muffin tin. All of a sudden an epiphany occurred, she retired the veteran muffin tin to the darkest corner of the pantry and began baking her muffin dough in a nice little no-stick 8"x8" square pan, having greased the pan anyway for auld lang syne. And that's how the muffins got to be tea bread and here's what you do.

Charlotte's Tea Bread

Set your oven at 400 degrees to warm it up, get out your mixing bowl and measure into it:

    1 cup all-purpose flour (unbleached)
    1 cup whole-wheat flour
    1 tsp. baking powder
    1/2 tsp. baking soda
    1/4 tsp. salt
    1 tsp. cinnamon
    1/4 tsp. nutmeg
    3 Tbsp. brown sugar (or 1 great, heaping glob of a Tbsp. if you're the sort who cooks by ear as Charlotte does)

No sifting is needed, just stir until the ingredients are well mixed. Add approximately 1/2 - 1 cup of raisins, depending on how well you like them. Ditto walnut meats, whole, chopped, or roughly broken as preferred. Stir into flour mixture; this will keep them from falling to the bottom of the pan in one sticky mess.
Into your measuring cup break 1 large egg.
Add 2 Tbsp. cooking oil and stir briskly until well mixed. Make a hole in the dry ingredients and pour in the egg mixture. Add 1-1/2 cups buttermilk (or soured milk). Stir all together just until all the dry ingredients are moistened and the dough sticks together. Do not beat any harder or longer than you have to...as any romance writer could tell you, it's a tender touch that brings on a happy

ending.

Oven temperatures may vary, no matter what they say. Charlotte suggests baking about 15 minutes, until the cake smells done, has pulled away from the sides of the pan, and leaves no sticky dough on a slim-bladed sharp knife or cake tester inserted down through the center of the cake. If you're not sure about the doneness, put it back in for another few minutes and test again.

This recipe is not the sort of fluffy, cake-like muffin or tea loaf that you find in commercial bakeries or coffee shops. Its texture is firm and substantial. It is high in nutrients, keeps well, freezes well assuming there's any left to freeze and may be eaten hot or cold, by itself or with butter, cheese, jam or whatever you like. Dates or other dried fruit may be substituted for raisins, and other unsalted nuts (not peanuts or cashews) for walnuts. Chacun à son goût. Bon appetit.

Margaret Maron

A past president of Sisters-in-Crime, Margaret Maron swept the mystery awards with The Bootlegger's Daughter, *the first of the Deborah Knott series, which received the Edgar, Agatha and Anthony awards. Her third in the series,* Shooting at Loons, *came out in the spring of 1994. She has also written seven books in the Lt. Sigrid Harald, NYPD series.*

In *Bootlegger's Daughter* there's been a coolness between Deborah Knott and her father. When they run into each other at the farm, Kezzie tries to tempt her to stay:

"Maidie's making me chicken pastry."
"Oh?" Chicken pastry was one of my favorite suppers.
"With chopped broccoli salad."
Another of my favorites. "You asking me to stay for supper?"
"Just saying there's plenty."
"You always did have a pretty way with words," I teased.

Once, when she was living "off" and got hungry for this Colleton County (N.C.) staple, Deborah phoned Maidie and asked her how to make it. Here's the way Maidie said to do it:

Maidie's Chicken Pastry

Take a nice fat stewing hen, cut it up and boil it in your biggest stew pot with a little salt till the meat's about to fall off the bones. Take off the good meat and put all the skin and bones back in the pot with 1 tsp. of celery seeds and keep boiling till you get a good rich broth. Strain out the skin and bones and put all the broth back in the pot and add enough water to half fill the pot.

"Skim off all the fat, right?" I asked.
"Little chicken grease never hurt nobody," said Maidie, sounding like one of Lev's kosher aunts. "Leave it on."

While the broth's heating back up to a good rolling boil, mix you up 4 cups of sifted plain flour and a little salt with 2 beaten eggs and enough water to make dough. You don't want it soft as biscuit dough, but you don't want it so stiff you can't work it good. Then roll it out real thin and cut it into strips about 3 fingers wide. Drop the strips in the boiling broth and leave the lid off till it's done and there's no more flour taste—about 15 minutes. Then you stir in the pieces of cooked chicken, heat it through and serve it up with something green.

"You eating enough greens?" Maidie asked.
It was something she asked every time I called that winter.
"Artichokes," I told her. "Asparagus. Alfalfa sprouts."
"I mean real greens," she sniffed. "Collards, turnip sallet."
She made me homesick.

Jack Matthews

The author of 21 books, including An Interview with the Sphinx *and* Storyhood as We Know It and Other Stories, *Jack Matthews has received a Guggenheim Fellowship and numerous awards. His stories, poems and essays have appeared in many reviews and periodicals such as* The Yale Review *and* The Sewanee Review.

Jackanapes Fricasee

2 cups rice
1 cup of cottage cheese
Cooked chicken breast
2-1/2 ounces black olives
Small onion
2 small jalapeno peppers
2 Tbsp. cilantro
2 Tbsp. olive oil
2 Tbsp. water

Steam rice.
Skin and dice chicken; dice onion and jalapenos. Mix with cilantro and dump all into a frying pan containing olive oil and water. Saute over low heat for 15 or 20 minutes, then add cottage cheese and let simmer for an additional 5 minutes. Serve over the boiled rice. Feeds 2. Parmesan cheese may be added to taste.
Note: ground beef or any other meat can, of course, be substituted for the chicken.

Sharyn McCrumb

Sharyn McCrumb, who has served as a member of the Appalachian Studies faculty at Virginia Tech, has won the Edgar, Agatha, and Macavity awards for her popular mysteries. Her novel, If Ever I Return, Pretty Peggy-O, *was named a* New York Times *Notable Book of 1990. Seven of her novels feature Elizabeth MacPherson, a forensic anthropologist sleuth. Elizabeth's latest adventure is* MacPherson's Lament *in which her brother, the novice attorney, is swindled by eight sweet old ladies from the Home for Confederate Women.*

Dear Bill,

I cannot think why you agreed to take a dessert to the Young Lawyers Social, unless the others want to get in a little practice suing for damages to their taste buds. I would have expected you to take your usual buffet staple: cartoon napkins and plastic forks, but then I suppose that your law partner, who could enter the Miss America contest as Ms Visigoth, probably bagged that contribution, and now you are driven to cook. Poor Bill.

Well, like the good sister that I am, I have managed to obtain for you a highly prestigious and coveted cake recipe. According to Cameron's mother, this recipe belongs to Queen Elizabeth herself, though when she finds time to cook I don't know. I hope you are properly impressed. Incidentally, Bill, you cannot do this in a toaster-oven. Try to find someone who has a real kitchen.

Here's the recipe.

Elizabeth MacPherson's Queen Elizabeth Cake

Take 1 cup of boiling water (Get someone to explain to you how to do this) and pour it over a cup of chopped dates. (The kind you buy in the grocery store, as opposed to the kind you don't have.) Add 1 tsp. of baking soda. Let that mixture stand while you mix the following ingredients. (The Queen probably has a scullery maid to do this:)

- 1 cup sugar
- 1/4 cup butter
- 1 beaten egg
- 1 tsp. vanilla
- 1/3 tsp. salt
- 1/3 cup chopped nuts

Add mixture to the date goo, alternating with 1-1/2 cups of flour with 1 tsp. baking powder. (There is a difference between baking soda and baking powder. We don't have to get philosophical about this as long as you use the one you're told to.) Pour the whole thing into an 8"x10" pan and bake in 375 degree oven for 35 minutes. (A bundt pan makes a nicely shaped cake, but I know that you think a bundt is a German political association, so never mind.)

Icing

You can top this cake with powdered sugar, if you are too lazy to actually make an icing. The rest of us combine 5 Tbsp. brown sugar, 3 Tbsp. butter, 3 Tbsp. milk. Boil 3 minutes, cool, beat until the mixture thickens.

If you can talk Mother into letting you use the Spode china and the family silver, the cake will be quite impressive—but since you will be serving this at a gathering of your fellow attorneys, be sure to count the forks.

According to Cameron's mother, the Queen requests that you

pay a "Royalty," each time you use her recipe, by donating one pound sterling to a charity. (That's about $1.55 at the moment.) You ought to send yours to the Legal Aid Society.

Bon appetit!

                    Your talented sister,
                    Elizabeth

Tim McLaurin

Tim McLaurin is a former Marine, Peace Corps volunteer, carpenter and professional snake handler. He is the author of two novels, The Acorn Plan *and* Woodrow's Trumpet, *and the highly acclaimed memoir* Keeper of the Moon. *His new novel,* Cured By Fire, *will be published by Putnam in January, 1995. He lives near Chapel Hill, North Carolina.*

Here are three recipes that I like to cook. All are fit for a pig picking.

Neck Bones and Noodles

5 pounds of pork neck bones
1 large yellow onion chopped coarsely
3 boxes of elbow macaroni
Salt and pepper to taste

Cook the neck bones and onion with salt and pepper for a couple of hours in a big pot. When the meat is tender, remove to a platter. Add the macaroni to the water in the pot and simmer until done. Adjust seasoning.
The macaroni noodles are easiest eaten from bowls, the juice sopped with cornbread. The neck bones are best eaten with the fingers and may be gnawed to get all the little pieces of meat. The finished bones can be chunked to one of the dogs that are sure to be begging.

Pan Fried Cornbread

Yellow corn meal
Water
Salt and pepper
Lard or corn oil

Mix the corn meal, seasoning and water until the batter is like thick mud. Drop large spoonfuls into a hot frying pan with 1/2" of oil in the bottom until the patties are about as big around as apples. Fry until the bottom is golden brown, then flip and cook the same on the other side until crisp on the outside and hot and gooey inside. Eat them hot. If you want to get fancy, you can add chopped onions or even jalapenos to the batter before cooking. Corn oil will add less calories and fat, but since you're already eating hog, you might as well use lard. Lard flavors the cornbread better.

Baked Cheese Grits with Garlic

This is an uptown way of fixing grits. You could eat this for Sunday dinner or use the dish to feed many hungry people at a party. Grits go a long way.

Regular grits (not the instant kind)
1 can beef broth
2 eggs
1 can cheddar cheese soup
Margarine
Milk
2 cloves garlic, minced
Salt and pepper

Cook grits in a mixture of water and beef broth. Mix the cooked grits with remaining ingredients and bake about an hour, or until the top is crusty and golden brown.
Even Yankees will eat grits cooked this way. If one balks, tell him it's made from Cream of Wheat.

Barbara Michaels

Barbara Michaels, who also writes as Elizabeth Peters, has a Ph.D. in Egyptology from the University of Chicago. She has been president of the American Crime Writers League and was named as the first Anthony Grand Master. Her novels include The Last Camel Died at Noon *and* The Curse of the Pharoahs.

Holiday Apricot Bars

2/3 cup dried apricots
1/2 cup soft butter
1/4 cup granulated sugar
1 cup sifted flour
1/3 cup sifted flour
1/2 tsp. baking powder
1/4 tsp. salt
1 cup brown sugar
2 eggs
1/2 tsp. vanilla
1/2 cup chopped nuts

Cook apricots for 10 minutes, drain and cool. Chop. Mix butter, sugar and 1 cup flour till crumbly. Press into 8" square pan, bake 25 minutes or till lightly browned. Sift 1/3 cup flour, baking powder, salt. Gradually beat brown sugar into well beaten eggs. Add sifted flour mixture and mix well. Add vanilla, nuts and apricots. Spread over baked layer. Bake 30 minutes. Cool in pan. Frost with powdered sugar frosting or roll in powdered sugar after cutting into bars. Makes 2-1/2 dozen. (Says who?)

Susan Oleksiw

A scholar of mystery novels as well as writer of them, Susan Oleksiw is the author two books featuring Police Chief Joe Silva—Doubletake, *and* Murder in Mellingham—*and* A Reader's Guide to the Classic British Mystery.

Joe Silva, chief of police in Mellingham, is of Portuguese descent and a meat-and-potatoes man (so, of course, he loves this sausage-and-eggplant recipe).

I've been cooking and freezing a variation of this recipe for the last month because we had a bumper crop of eggplant in our garden this summer. I make up my recipes as I go along, so every cook should feel free to vary what I offer here.

Portuguese Sausage and Eggplant Casserole

2 Linguica (mild Portuguese sausage)
2 Chaurico (spicy Portuguese sausage)
1 large onion diced
5 large tomatoes cut in wedges
2 green peppers sliced
2 cups chopped kale
1/4 tsp. paprika
1 tsp. salt
1 medium eggplant pared and cut into small cubes
1 cup grated cheese

Saute the onion slightly. Brown the sausages in the onion and set aside. In a large pot add the tomatoes, peppers, kale, salt, and paprika. Simmer until the tomatoes are soft and starting to fall apart. Add the eggplant and mix gently. Cut the sausages into bite-size pieces. Add to the eggplant mixture. Turn into a buttered casserole dish. Sprinkle the top with grated cheese. Bake 45 minutes covered at 350 degrees. Bake uncovered until top browns. Serve with crusty Italian bread and a green salad. Serves 4.

Sara Paretsky

Sara Paretsky's series of mysteries featuring female detective V.I. Warshawski, the most recent of which is Tunnel Vision, *have been enormously popular. A founder of Sisters in Crime, she lives in Chicago with her husband and their golden retriever.*

This is a dish which Gabriella Sestieri Warshawski would make for her family if people were under the weather—she believed the broccoli gave special vitamins while the eggs were good nourishment for colds or flu. V. I. will make this frittata when she's down in the dumps and wants to recreate the sense of nurturing she got from her mother.

Frittata Gabriella

Fresh broccoli florets
1 small onion
4-6 mushrooms
4 eggs
Grated cheddar cheese

Boil the broccoli for 1-2 minutes (shorter if you like it crisp, longer if you like it soft). Remove immediately from water, drain, and rinse under cold water.
Turn on the broiler.
Saute the onion and mushrooms over low heat in about 2 Tbsp. olive oil. When they are cooked, add the broccoli to the pan. Beat the eggs lightly. Add 1 tsp. of water to the eggs. Pour over the vegetables and cook on low to medium heat until the eggs are

golden brown on the bottom. Put cheese on the top and stick pan under broiler until cheese and eggs are a golden brown. Eat with chewy Italian bread and a bottle of Barolo. Serves 2.

Nancy Pickard

Creator of the Jenny Cain mystery series, Nancy Pickard has won the Agatha, Macavity, Anthony, and American Mystery awards. She tapped her 14 years of ranching experience for her novel The 27-Ingredient Chili Con Carne Mystery, *which she based on the characters and storyline by the late Virginia Rich, who wrote three Eugenia Potter mysteries before her death in 1984. Eugenia Potter was known as the "Culinary Queen of Crime."*

Eugenia Potter's 27-Ingredient Chili Con Carne

1 lb. dry pinto beans
1/2 cup chopped sweet red pepper
1/2 cup chopped green pepper
1/2 cup butter or margarine
1 9-oz. can pitted ripe olives, chopped
2 medium onions, chopped
1 7-oz. can diced green chilies
1/2 cup minced parsley
2 cloves garlic, minced
1 12-oz. bottle chili sauce
3 lbs. chopped sirloin
1 lb. pork sausage
1 Tbsp. salt
1 Tbsp. garlic salt
2 Tbsp. flour
2 tsp. black pepper
1 1-lb. can baked beans

  1 Tbsp. chopped cilantro
  1 4-oz. can pimientos
  1 Tbsp. oregano
  2 30-oz. cans tomatoes
  2-4 Tbsp. chili powder, to taste
  3/4 cup chopped celery
  Grated orange peel
  1/2 lb. sliced fresh mushrooms
  1 pt. sour cream

Wash and drain pinto beans and soak in water overnight. Bring to boil, lower heat, and simmer 2-3 hours or until tender. Drain. Meanwhile, melt butter in large skillet and add onions, chilies, and garlic. Saute until onion is soft. Add chopped sirloin and cook over moderate heat until meat is brown. In a separate pan brown sausage and pour off fat. Add sausage to meat mixture. Sprinkle with flour and stir to blend, then transfer to Dutch oven or 8-quart kettle. Add pinto and canned beans and all remaining ingredients except sour cream; bring just to boil. Lower heat and simmer about 30 minutes. Skim off fat with a cold spoon as it rises to the top. Serve with sour cream. Serves 20.
Freezes wonderfully.

Chef Dennis's Albondigas Soup

In mixing bowl, mix 2 lbs. lean ground beef, 1/2 teaspoon garlic powder, 1/2 teaspoon ground cumin, pinch of oregano and pinch of cilantro. Shape ingredients into 1-oz. meatballs. In a large pot, saute in 3 oz. of butter: 1 cup diced tomatoes, 1/2 cup diced green chilies, 4 cloves chopped garlic, 2 medium chopped onions, 1 lb. chopped green cabbage, 1 finely diced medium zucchini, and 1/2 bunch cilantro. Add 3 quarts beef broth. Just before broth comes to a boil, add the meatballs, one at a time. Add salt and black pepper to taste. Simmer for 30 minutes. Top with chopped cilantro just before serving. Serves 12 to 15. This is even better the next day.

Salsa Mexicana

Mix 5 canned green chilies, diced, with 5 large tomatoes, peeled and finely chopped. Add 1 or 2 cloves minced garlic, 1 minced onion, 1 Tbsp. chopped fresh cilantro, 1 Tbsp. vinegar, and 1 Tbsp. oil. Mix. Season with salt and black pepper to taste. Serve with blue corn chips.

Juanita Ortega's Chili Rellenos

In a 9"x12" casserole, continuously layer 3 small cans whole chilies, split and laid flat, 3/4 lb. grated Monterey Jack cheese, and 3/4 lb. grated longhorn cheese until all indredients are used, ending with cheese on top. Mix in blender 3 whole eggs, 3 tablespoons flour, and 1 6-oz. can condensed milk. Pour mixture over chili-and-cheese casserole. Bake in 350 degree oven for 30 minutes. Top with 6-oz. can taco sauce and bake 30 minutes more.

Che Thomas's Guacamole

With a fork, mash 2 large ripe avocados into coarse pulp while blending in 2 or 3 tablespoons lemon or lime juice. Add 1/2 tsp. salt and 2-4 canned chilies, chopped. Makes about 1-1/2 cup guacamole. Serve with chips.

Capirotada (Mexican Bread Pudding)

To 1 quart boiling water add 2 cups brown sugar, 1 whole clove, 1 stick of cinnamon, and 1/4 cup butter. Simmer until a light syrup forms, then remove the clove and cinnamon. Cut 1 loaf raisin bread into cubes and dry in 250 degree oven until crusty. Rinse 1 cup raisins in hot water, then drain. In a large buttered baking dish, continuously layer the bread cubes, raisins, 1 cup chopped walnuts, 1/4 lb. Monterey Jack cheese, and 1/4 lb. longhorn cheese until all ingredients are used. Spoon the hot syrup evenly over the bread mixture. Bake in a preheated oven at 350 degrees for 30 minutes. Serve either hot or cold. Serves 6-8.

Belva Plain

Belva Plain's bestselling novels include Treasures, Whispers *and the most recent,* Daybreak. Evergreen *was produced as a miniseries by NBC. Plain also has published short stories in* McCalls, Good Housekeeping, Redbook *and* Cosmopolitan.

Cheesecake

2 lbs. cream cheese
1 pt. of sweet cream
Juice of one lemon or 2 Tbsp. of RealLemon
2 Tbsp. vanilla
7 eggs
1-1/2 cups sugar
2 Tbsp. flour

Cream together the cream cheese and sugar; do it very thoroughly. One at a time, and gradually, add the unbeaten eggs, the lemon juice, vanilla, flour, and the unbeaten cream. Bake at 350 degrees in a greased 9" or 10" spring-form pan for 65 minutes. Then turn off the oven and let the cake set in the closed oven for 2 hours.

Dawn Raffel

Dawn Raffel's fiction has appeared in Iowa Review, North American Review *and others. In the Year of Long Division, a collection of short stories, will be published in January 1995. Raffel is books and fiction editor of* Redbook.

My book is filled with images of snow and ice, so it's only fitting to offer a recipe for something frozen. This is my grandmother's ice box cake:

Ice Box Cake

3 square dark baking chocolate, melted and cooled
1/4 cup cold water mixed with 1-1/2 half pkg. of gelatine, then mixed with boiling water to total 1 cup, then cooled
6 eggs
1-1/2 cups sugar
1 tsp. vanilla
1 angel food cake (between 1 and 1-1/2 pounds)
1 pt. whipped cream

Beat the egg whites with half of the sugar, then beat the yolks with the other half of the sugar and the vanilla. Add the beaten yolk mixture to the cooled chocolate and cooled gelatin, then add the stiff egg whites. Break up the angel food cake and mix gently with the other ingredients. Put into a greased torte pan and refrigerate for 8 hours. Frost with whipped cream.

Naomi Ragen

An American who has lived in Jerusalem for more than 20 years working as a journalist and freelance writer, Naomi Ragen is the author of Jephte's Daughter *and* Sotah: A Novel.

Below you will find Leah Harshen's (Bathsheva HaLevi's endearing mother-in-law from *Jephte's Daughter*) Jerusalem Kugel recipe (made fresh for Shabbat, as it should be by good Jewish daughters-in-law, who wouldn't dream of buying it frozen like certain lazy good-for-nothing Americans...)

Jerusalem Kugel

1 lb. medium fine noodles
1/2 cup oil
1 cup sugar
4 eggs, beaten
1-1/2 tsp. salt
1-2 tsp. pepper, to taste

Boil noodles in a large pot of salted water for 5 minutes. Drain, but do not rinse. Caramelize sugar by pouring oil and 3/4 cup sugar into a heavy pot. Stir occasionally over medium-low heat (this is the hardest part, so pay attention; don't read books or dream, or it will burn black, and you'll wind up throwing it out: waste, terrible waste!!) When sugar just begins to melt and bubble and turn a lovely golden hue, pour immediately over hot noodles. Stir in eggs, remaining sugar, salt, and pepper. Line a 4- or 5-qt. pot with wax paper. Pour in noodle mixture. Cover and bake in a preheated

325 degree oven for 1-1/2 hours. To keep warm over Shabbat, leave on covered stove top, called a blech, or hot plate overnight until ready to serve for Shabbat lunch. Serves 10-12.

Sandra Redding

Sandra Redding's short stories have appeared in many anthologies, including the bestselling When I Am an Old Woman I Shall Wear Purple. *A resident of Greensboro, North Carolina, she teaches writing at Guilford Technical Community College and publishes articles and reviews in newspapers and magazines.*

Once a group of soldiers camped outside the gates of an unfamiliar town. Though their stomachs and pockets were empty, their imaginations were richly endowed, so they placed a stone in a large kettle and set it to boiling. Soon curious townspeople stopped, asked what they were cooking.

"Soup," the soldiers told them, and if you add vegetables to the pot, we'll share with you.

One after the other, the townspeople came, bringing food to add to the pot. Soon the soup was perfectly cooked. Sitting down together, all the soldiers and townspeople ate until their stomachs could hold no more.

Stone Soup

Based on the stone soup legend, my recipe is the perfect concoction for the destitute writer who's spent her last royalty check and doesn't know when another will be forthcoming. No need to eat dog food and suffer alone. Just emulate the wise soldiers: find a rock, clean it up, place it in the bottom of a large pot, cover with water, and simmer.

Invite writer friends; request that they each bring a can of beans, tomatoes, corn, peas or a pack of noodles. Dump whatever food that shows up into the pot. If you feel extravagant, place two pounds of pre-cooked stew beef along with broth in with the rest of the stuff. Let all ingredients simmer while you and your company drink the bottles of wine (or other libation) someone will surely bring.

    Then about an hour later, you'll have a soup to serve your guests. Perhaps not an M.F.K. Fisher gastronomic wonder, but communing and celebrating with friends will make it one fine party anyway.

    Recipe serves: all who show up.

Judith Richards

Judith Richards' novel Summer Lightning *was published in 15 languages, was condensed by* Readers Digest *and was a selection of the Literary Guild. It has been optioned by Disney Studios. Richards, who is the author of three other novels, lives in Alabama with her husband, Terry Cline, also a writer.*

Judith's Tacos

10 taco shells
3/4 lb. ground beef
1 tsp. lemon juice
Salt to taste
1/8 tsp. pepper
1/2 tsp. cumin
2 tsp. chili powder
3/4 cup refried beans
3/4 cup onions, chopped
2 cups lettuce, shredded
1 cup cheddar cheese, shredded
1 cup tomatoes, diced (optional)
Salsa

Set oven at 250 to heat shells while you prepare other ingredients. Place shells (upside down—i.e., open side down) on cookie sheet. Set timer for 30 minutes. (If your oven heats unevenly, check the shells in 15 minutes. to be sure they aren't burned.)
Gather ingredients needed to fill the taco...cheese, lettuce, tomato and onion. Grate cheese and place in refrigerator. Finely chop

onions, shred lettuce into tiny pieces, and dice tomatoes. Set aside in separate bowls.

If shells have been in oven 20 minutes, prepare beef filling. Place ground beef in medium size saucepan. Use large spoon to break it up. Season with chili powder, cumin, salt, pepper, and lemon juice. Cook beef on low heat with lid on the pan. Every couple of minutes, use big spoon to break the meat into fine little pieces.

Put refried beans in small saucepan with a tablespoon of water and heat on very low temperature, with the lid on pan. Stir frequently. Meanwhile the beef should be sauteed long enough to brown and cook through. Don't overcook. Beans require only a few minutes to heat through. You are ready to serve tacos.

I fill my taco shell in this order: beef, beans, onions, lettuce, cheese, tomatoes, making thin layers of each. I like some extra lettuce and tomatoes or slices of bell pepper on the side to prop up the taco and to serve as salad.

The salsa is added last, spooned over the top layer of the taco to seep down and blend all those flavors.

Crispy shells and lemon juice are my secrets to the best tacos you ever ate.

Serve with limeade (or a marguerita) for a tasty accent.

Any fruit-flavored light dessert, such as pineapple sherbet, will top off this meal.

Les Roberts

A screenwriter before taking up mystery writing and winning the Private Eye Writers of America's Award for best first novel for An Infinite Number of Monkeys, *Les Roberts has produced the Saxon series, set in Los Angeles, and the Milan Jacovich series, set in Cleveland. He is writing the screenplay for a film based on his novel,* Pepper Pike, *which will star Scott Bakula as Milan.*

Milan Jacovich's "Chicken Village" Chicken Paprikash

Take 3 large onions, chopped as fine as possible. Put in a heavy pan with 1 Tbsp. of Crisco. Cook VERY slowly over a low heat for about an hour until it reaches a jelly-like consistency. Add 1 Tbsp. Hungarian paprika and a pinch of cayenne pepper (to taste). Simmer for 10 minutes.
Add 2 cut-up roasting chickens, cover well, and stew for half an hour.
Add 2 coarsely diced red bell peppers (seeded), salt to taste, and stew another half hour.
Add 2 Tbsp. sweet cream and 1 tsp. flour.
THE SECOND IT STARTS TO BOIL, remove it. Don't wait a moment longer.
Serve with dumplings or egg noodles. Serves 4.

Tim Sandlin

A cook at the Lame Duck Chinese restaurant in Jackson, Wyoming, Tim Sandlin is known as "The Wizard of the Far Western Weird." His tales are wickedly funny and show a Saroyanesque love for human comedy. His books include Skipped Parts *and* Sorrow Floats.

This recipe was told to me by a dying Kickapoo Indian on an iceflow. Before he went over the falls, he said he had to pass on the ancient tribal chili recipe so that it would not die with him. Dancing With Gophers' recipe calls for antelope burger, but I have found it works well with any ground game, regular lean hamburger, or even turkey burger.

Kickapoo Chili

2 lbs. lean hamburger
add microwave jackrabbit*
4 onions chopped semi-fine (or well)
2 Tbsp. chili powder
1 Tbsp. cumin

Simmer until burger is browned, then drain the excess fat.

Add:
2 cans Wolf Brand chili. (Dancing With Gophers was specific about the brand, but any canned chili without beans works. Kickapoos hate canned beans.)
2 cans whole tomatoes (When adding the tomatoes, place

each tomato in your palm and squeeze, allowing the pulp to flow between your fingers into the chili. This gives a much better consistency than cutting them up. The priggish can cut them.)

As the juice simmers, add another 2 Tbsp. chili powder, 1 Tbsp. cumin. Simmer to chili thickness.

*The original tribal recipe calls for a jackrabbit but I generally leave it out. Few guests enjoy hare in their food.

Eve Sandstrom

A columnist for the Lawton, Oklahoma Constitution, *Eve Sandstrom is a fourth-generation Oklahoman whose Choctaw ancestors arrived in the state before the Civil War. Her first mystery,* Death Down Home, *won the best novel award from the Oklahoma Federation of Writers. She also is author of* The Down Home Heifer Heist.

    Like all busy people, I'm always delighted to find an easy, delicious meal that can be prepared ahead of time. Luckily, I married into just such a dish.

    This recipe was passed on to me by my mother-in-law, Ruth H. Sandstrom, who today lives in Orlando, Florida. I assemble it the night before, set the oven timer, stick the pot in before I leave for work and come home to a hot dinner.

Gigi's Bean Pot Stew

1 lb. stew meat, cut in 1-inch chunks.
Carrots, cut in chunks
Onions, cut in chunks
Salt and pepper
1 can tomato soup
Water to cover

Mix all ingredients in a bean pot or other heavy casserole. Bake 3 or 4 hours at 325 degrees. If this needs thickening at the end, shake up 2 Tbsp. flour in 1/2 cup water and add. We serve it over mashed potatoes. Stuffed celery makes a nice side dish.
This can be done in a crock pot, but I believe the flavor is a little better if it's baked.

John Saul

For a few years, John Saul traveled about the country writing and supporting himself with odd jobs. After settling in Seattle, he was director of Seattle Theater Arts before beginning his successful series of bestselling horror novels, including Darkness *and* Shadows.

I could tell you about the recipe for turtle soup which I always enjoyed reading. It started with "...get yourself a green turtle and a hatchet. Wait until he sticks his head out and then chop it off!" But I won't.

The recipe I will share with you is one I serve all the time in my home in the San Juan Islands in the state of Washington. I call it Crabby-Wabby Casserole (don't ask why).

Crabby-Wabby Casserole

3-4 cups of cooked white rice
1 cup cooked peas
2 cups cooked dungeness crab meat
1/2 onion, chopped
4 green onions, chopped
Approximately 3 Tbsp. pimentos, also chopped, of course!
1/4 lb, butter
At least 1/2 cup grated Parmesan cheese

Preheat oven to 400 degrees.
Mix the rice, peas, onion, green onion, crab and pimentos in a large casserole dish. Dot the top with the butter, then cover the whole thing with parmesan cheese.

Bake, uncovered, for 15-30 minutes, or until top is slightly brown and the casserole is heated all the way through. Serve with salad and garlic bread. Can be reheated in microwave.

Louise Shivers

Louise Shivers' first novel, Here to Get My Baby Out of Jail, *drew critical acclaim and comparisons with Flannery O'Connor and Eudora Welty. Her second novel,* Whistling Woman, *recently released, also gathered rave reviews.*

Georgeanna is the main character of *A Whistling Woman*. For her wedding, Maebelle made this special nut cake from one of Mrs. Fleeting's old recipes.

The Walnut Wedding Cake

4-1/4 cups flour
2 cups plus 1 Tbsp. sugar
1/2 lb. butter
1/4 lb. candied cherries
7 eggs
4 cups nuts, half black walnuts, half pecans
2 tsp. nutmeg
1/2 cup whiskey or brandy
1 tsp. baking powder
2 boxes white raisins (golden)

Sift flour several times, measure, add baking powder and nutmeg. Sift over chopped nuts combined with raisins.
Cream butter and sugar, beat well, adding 1 egg at the time. Add whiskey, beat well, add flour, nuts, etc. mixture a little at the time beating thoroughly until all is added. (There is no beating to this mixture, it is so thick.) I mix mine in a dish pan and sometimes

even use my hand, or a very large spoon, to mix it thoroughly.
Pour into a well-greased funnel pan which has been lined with several thicknesses of waxed paper on bottom and sides.
Bake in moderate oven at 250 degrees for 2 hours. Have pan of water under cake. (If you have a hot or good heating oven, you had better watch it and turn it down lower as this cake cooks fast.) This makes a thick cake and is hard to cook through sometimes.

Anne Rivers Siddons

Since her first book, John Chancellor Makes Me Cry, *Anne Rivers Siddons has published nine more novels, most bestsellers, including* Colony, Outer Banks *and her most recent,* Downtown. *She lives in Atlanta.*

Three generations of my family have served these oysters on Christmas Eve as an entree, usually with a green salad dressed with oil and lemon juice and served with a crusty French bread. Citrus ambrosia makes a good dessert, and a dry white wine is a nice accompaniment.

Christmas Eve Scalloped Oysters

2 qt. freshly shucked oysters
1 stick unsalted butter
1 pkg. saltine crackers
2 cups fresh grated Parmesan cheese
Worcestershire sauce
Dry sherry
White pepper
Tabasco sauce
1 pt. Half & Half
Liquor from oysters

Drain oysters over sieve, reserving liquor. In a mixing bowl, combine the Half & Half and enough oyster liquor to make 2 cups liquid; add a dash of Worcestershire sauce, a generous slosh of sherry (maybe 1/4 cup), and a small dash of Tabasco. Mix well. In a large casserole, make a layer of oysters to cover bottom.

Crumble saltines over it to make a fairly thick layer of cracker pieces. Scatter grated Parmesan cheese over the crackers. Dust with pepper. Repeat twice more, finishing with cracker and cheese layer.

With a long teaspoon or skewer, make several holes in the casserole deep enough so that the utensil touches the bottom of the dish. Pour liquid mixture over casserole until it appears around the edges of the oyster-cracker mixture.

Bake uncovered at 325 degrees until entire casserole bubbles. This could take from 30 minutes to an hour depending on the depth of the dish. Give it enough time.

Elizabeth Spencer

Born and reared in Mississippi, Elizabeth Spencer, who now teaches writing at the University of North Carolina at Chapel Hill, spent many years in Italy, the setting for several of her books, including The Light in the Piazza, *which was made into a movie. Among her other books are* The Night Travelers *and* On the Gulf. *Her play,* For Lease or Sale, *was first produced by Playmakers Repertory Company in Chapel Hill.*

This is from the recipes of my dear friend Elizabeth Willis, one of the world's best cooks. I myself happen not to like green peppers, so I know that a substitution of red peppers is acceptable. The eggplant is delicious with a full dress turkey dinner or baked ham.

Eggplant Creole

2 medium eggplant
3 Tbsp. butter
3 Tbsp. flour
3 cups canned tomatoes, chopped
2 small green peppers, seeded and chopped
2 medium onions, chopped
1 tsp. salt
2 Tbsp. brown sugar
3 bay leaves
5 or 6 whole cloves
1/2 cup slivered almonds, toasted
1 cup grated cheddar cheese
Bread crumbs to cover

Peel and dice eggplant. Boil in salted water for about 10 minutes. Drain and place in greased baking dish.

Melt butter, add flour and stir until lightly brown. Add tomatoes, peppers, onions, salt, brown sugar, bay leaves and cloves. Cook slowly for 10 minutes. Add toasted almonds and pour over eggplant. Sprinkle cheese over all, then cover with bread crumbs and dot with butter.

Bake at 350 degrees for about 30 minutes. Can be made a day ahead and rebaked.

My favorite recipe for a dessert is my grandmother's, Elizabeth Young McCain's. It is called Golden Dream.

Golden Dream

Beat the yolks of 4 eggs slightly and add 2/3 cup of sugar, the juice of 1 orange. Grate rind of 1/4 of it, also juice of 1 lemon. Cook in a double boiler until thick, then fold in whites of the eggs beaten stiff. Cook a couple of minutes and if desired 2 tsp. dissolved gelatin may be added and the whole poured into a mold. Chill until firm. Top with whipped cream.

For me the gelatin is necessary, and I find it advisable to stir it into the hot mixture before the egg whites. Thus it has a better chance to thoroughly dissolve.

Elizabeth Daniels Squire

Elizabeth Daniels Squire's newspaper heritage goes back to her grandfather, editor and one-time Secretary of the Navy Josephus Daniels. Her father, Jonathan Daniels, was Harry S. Truman's press secretary; she herself has written for papers from Connecticut to Beirut and is on the board of the family-owned News and Observer *Company in Raleigh, North Carolina. She is the author of three mystery novels, including* Who Killed What's-Her-Name?, *featuring Peaches Dann, the absent-minded detective.*

Peaches suggests that when, in the throes of plotting a novel or composing a poem they forget worldly things, creative types should not berate themselves but cook something good instead. She believes in using getting-around-a-bad-memory tricks not only to solve crimes but also to make life more rewarding.

For anyone with a real sweet tooth, she recommends this Sweet Creativity Coffee Cake in two versions. Here's how to make it on a good day when you've done everything right and thus deserve a special treat.

Sweet Creativity Coffee Cake

Preheat oven to 350 degrees.
Sift together: 2 cups flour, 3 heaping tsp. baking powder, 1 tsp. cinnamon and a pinch of salt.
In a mixer blend: 1 Tbsp. butter, 1 cup light brown sugar, 2 whole

eggs.

To the dry ingredients add the egg mixture alternately with 3/4 cup milk.

Pour batter into a buttered shallow 8"x10" pan and bake about 20 minutes or until it shrinks from sides of pan. Watch after about 18 minutes.

While the cake is baking, blend over very low heat: 1 stick butter, 1 firmly packed cup brown sugar. Stir until the sugar is melted and the butter and sugar are entirely melded.

When the cake leaves the sides of the pan, take it out of the oven and poke holes in it with the handle of a wooden spoon. Pour on the melted topping which will flow into the holes as well as ice the top of the cake. Sprinkle with cinnamon and pkg. of chopped walnuts.

Put back in the oven with heat off for 5 minutes. Keeps well and freezes well. Always serve warm. Warm it covered with foil in a slow oven.

Nonfiction buffs may like to know that this was a favorite with historian Hendrick Willem Van Loon. The woman who gave this recipe to Peaches' creator, Liz Squire, often made it for him.

On a forget-everything day when you lose your glasses, lock yourself out, and forget to put the groceries away, Peaches suggests you make this cake, or almost any other baked goods by the Updated Grandma's Sour Milk Rule. This rule is the result of research. Peaches believes firmly in research, which is why she's used the "world memory" or international network of newspaper library computers to help her find a killer.)

Updated Grandma's Sour Milk Rule

Your grandmother's or great grandmother's cookbook was full of recipes for baking with sour milk. In their day, milk soured naturally. Now it's stabilized. First it's good. Then it's on-the-verge. Then it goes so bad it's not good for baking.

If you have had practice forgetting to put the milk in the fridge, you will easily recognize that on-the-verge-or-going-bad taste. It's not really unpleasant, just not quite right. Immediately add 1-1/3 Tbsp. of vinegar or 1-1/2 Tbsp. of lemon juice for each cup you're going to use for baking.

To complete the leavening process, replace the baking powder in a recipe with a 1/2 tsp. of baking soda for each 2 cups of flour. Sift with dry ingredients. That's important. For Sweet Creativity Coffee Cake, which needs a lot of leavening, also include 1 tsp. of baking powder.

So on an I-forgot-the-milk day, make coffee cake or pancakes, or biscuits, or some of grandma's favorites, the old fashioned sour-milk way, with a twist to fit modern milk. You certainly deserve a special treat!

Allen Steele

The author of several noted science fiction novels, most recently Labyrinth of Night *and* The Jericho Iteration, *Allen Steele has won the Locus and the Donald A. Wollheim awards. He lives in St. Louis with his wife and two dogs, and does most of the cooking (he's still training the dogs.)*

Most of my recipes are either rather pedestrian, meat-and-potatoes stuff (meatloaf, scrambled eggs, London Broil, etc.) or so experimental that I reserve them for my wife and me, lest anyone sue me for inducing salmonella. This one, however, is literally "off the wall."

It's a lousy recipe, but it's damned effective for settling domestic quarrels.

Off The Wall Pizza

1 12" frozen pizza

Remove pizza from unrecyclable box and plastic wrapper. Do not attempt to cook or eat the pizza; most likely it is laden with preservatives which are bad for you.

Grasp the pizza much the way you would a Frisbee and, in single sideways motion, sling it in the direction of the person in your household whose turn it was to prepare a decent dinner but blew it off to watch TV instead.

For best results, use a pizza which has been in the freezer for at least 4 weeks. At this point, it is not only inedible, but has also acquired the stiffness necessary for satisfactory aeronautical performance. Wind tunnel tests indicate that one can reach velocities in excess of 15 mph, give or take a good tailwind.

Pizza in unthawed condition will probably survive initial impact with the kitchen wall. Although most of the toppings will have been dislodged, its crust will remain intact; chemical analysis shows that it is composed of a non-organic substance unknown to modern science. This structural integrity therefore allows the person who has been targeted to retrieve the alleged food product and, in a state of inchoate rage, hurl it back in your direction.

Repeat process until the pizza is throughly destroyed. Sulk for 10 minutes, then apologize for 30. Feed remains to the dogs, clean up the kitchen, and go out to dinner at a Chinese restaurant. Use of obscenities and gratuitous insults is optional. Not recommended for children, wealthy relatives, or spouses with a better sense of aim than your own.

Deborah Tannen

Deborah Tannen's You Just Don't Understand *was translated into 17 languages and has been a major bestseller in eight countries. Dr. Tannen has written seven other books—*Talking From 9 to 5 *has just been published—and edited eight others. She is on the Linguistics Department faculty at Georgetown University and has lectured throughout the world.*

I don't cook much, but some years ago I did occasionally, and then I usually cooked Greek dishes, some of which I learned to prepare from my first mother-in-law, Mathilde Paterakis. She lived on the Greek island of Crete, but was born in Smyrna (now Izmir, Turkey), which she left as a refugee from the Asia Minor Disaster in 1922, when Greeks were forced to flee Turkey.

I adored her, and have missed her terribly ever since her son and I split (amicably). I saw her only a few times after that, before she died in 1991. In memory of her, I offer this recipe for moussaka, the dish I most liked to prepare.

I don't remember whether this specific recipe came from her or not; I suspect it didn't, since she tended to prepare moussaka with potatoes. But Greek cooking always reminds me of her anyway.

It makes me think of her tiny kitchen in Crete, where she prepared elaborate meals of the food her husband brought home (He did not permit her to go to the market, which was only a few blocks from their home), and I recall how I often said to her, *Mirizis orea* ("You smell wonderful"), and she'd always reply, self deprecatingly, *Mirizo kouzina* ("I smell of the kitchen"), which was exactly right and exactly what I loved.

I am copying this recipe from an old index card on which I wrote it, half in English, half Greek. Here I translate it all into English. The measures are in kilos rather than pounds. I'd written some equivalents on my notes and give them, too.

Moussaka

1 kilo 280 grams (2-1/2 lbs) eggplants
670 grams (1-1/2 lbs.) chopmeat (in Greece this would be lamb, but beef is acceptable)
1/2 cup butter
1/2 cup grated cheese (in Greece it would be *kefalotiri*)
1/2 cup white wine
1 cup bread crumbs
2 Tbsp. grated onion
2 cups parsley (this may seem excessive to American palates; decrease if you wish)
670 grams (1-1/2 lbs.) tomatoes
Béchamel (recipe follows)
Olive oil for frying
Salt
Pepper

Put the meat and half the butter in a pot with the onion to brown. Mix and add a little wine. Add tomatoes, parsley, salt, and pepper, and let it drink all the water. Wash 1 eggplant, slice thin, and fry in oil with a little butter. Add salt and pepper after removal from pan.
Prepare the béchamel.
In a roasting pan, make layers of the eggplant, meat mixture, and half the bread crumbs and cheese. Pour the béchamel over the top, then sprinkle the remaining bread crumbs and cheese on top of that. Bake for 30-40 minutes in a medium oven.

Béchamel

6 Tbsp. butter

7 or 8 Tbsp. flour
4 cups milk
1-2 egg yolks
Salt
Pepper

Heat (but don't boil) milk. Put butter in a pot to melt. Add flour little by little and mix with a wooden spoon. Add heated milk little by little, mixing continually. Return pot to fire. Mix and cook until it thickens and becomes like cream. Remove from fire and add salt, pepper, and well-beaten egg yolks. If not used immediately, mix from time to time.

Patricia Taylor

A writer and photographer, Patricia Taylor is the author of four books on gardening, including Weekend Gardener's Guide *and* Easy Care Perennials. *She also writes on gardening for such publications as the* New York Times *and* Woman's Day. *She lives in Princeton, N.J. with her husband and two daughters.*

Curried Green Tomatoes

4 Tbsp. butter
1 medium onion, diced
4 medium green tomatoes, cut into bite-size chunks
2 Tbsp. curry (or less according to taste)

Melt butter in frying pan, add onion and simmer uncovered about 10 minutes until onions are golden. Turn off heat.
Add green tomatoes and sprinkle with curry. Cover. This part may be prepared up to 2 hours before serving.
Just before serving, turn heat on low. Simmer, covered, for about 5 minutes—enough to warm the tomatoes without turning them mushy.
This is delicious with mounds of hot cooked rice. Serves 4.

Mild Gazpacho

1 large (16-oz.) tomato, peeled
1/2 cucumber, peeled
1 small onion, peeled

1/2 green pepper, seeded
24-oz. can of tomato juice
1/4 tsp. powdered garlic or juice of 2 garlic cloves
1/3 cup olive oil
1/6 cup red wine vinegar

Put first 4 ingredients in a blender or food processor and liquify. If you like, these processed vegetables can be frozen until ready to be used.
Add vegetables to tomato juice. Combine last 3 ingredients; blend well and add to juice mixture.
Serve in drinking glasses or soup bowls at room temperature or chilled. This is a good substitute for alcoholic drinks and is refreshing with cheese and crackers and other hors d'oeuvres. Serves 6.

Tomato and Pasta Salad

4 lbs. ripe tomatoes, peeled, seeded, and diced
1/2 tsp powdered garlic or juice of 4 garlic cloves
1 tsp. dried basil or 20 fresh basil leaves, chopped fine
1/2 cup olive oil
1/2 lb. mozzarella cheese, diced
2 green peppers, seeded and cut in strips
1 lb. macaroni, preferably twists, cooked in boiling water and drained

Combine first 4 ingredients up to 3 hours before serving. Do not refrigerate.
About 1 hour before serving, add next 3 ingredients and salt and pepper to taste. Let sit about 1 hour at room temperature, stirring occasionally. Serves 8.

Vegetable Beef Soup

If you're on a diet, make this the day before, refrigerate, and then skim off all fat before reheating.

1 lb. hamburger
6 cups water
6 beef bouillon cubes
3 medium carrots, diced
2 ribs celery, diced
1 medium onion, diced
2 cups fresh tomatoes, peeled and chopped or 1 16-oz. can whole tomatoes
1/8 tsp. garlic powder or 1 garlic clove, diced fine
1 bay leaf
1 cup fresh or 1 pkg. frozen peas

Combine first 3 ingredients. Break up hamburger in cold water and then bring to a boil.

Add next 6 ingredients. Reduce heat, cover, and simmer for about 20 minutes.

Add peas and cook another 10 to 15 minutes. Serves 6.

Marilyn Wallace

Marilyn Wallace's first Goldstein and Cruz mystery, A Case of Loyalties, *won the Macavity Award for best first novel. The editor of the Sisters In Crime anthologies, she also is the author of* The Seduction *and* So Shall You Reap.

Because I lived in Brooklyn, Flemington, New Jersey, and Charlotte and Greensboro, North Carolina, as a child, I consider myself an honorary New Yorker, New Jerseyite, and, of course, a Tarheel. But when it comes to food, I claim status as an honorary Italian.

Mystery writers often play the game of "What if?" and one of my versions is, "What if I had to choose one of the world's wonderful cuisines?" The answer is always the same. How could I think of giving up olive oil, garlic, osso bucco, lasagna, pesto sauce, minestrone, zabaglione, pizza with sausage, tiramisu? And, especially, how would I ever manage without a demitasse of rich espresso and biscotti?

Mama Marilyn's Biscotti

1/4 lb. butter
1 tsp. anise seed
1 tsp. vanilla
1/2 tsp. almond extract
2-1/2 cup almonds
3-1/2 cup unbleached flour
3/4 tsp. baking powder
Pinch salt

3 eggs
1-1/4 cup sugar

Melt butter in small saucepan. Add anise seed. When cool, add vanilla, almond extract.
Combine almonds and 1/2 cup flour and slice in food processor using on-off pulses. Sift remaining flour with baking powder and salt.
Separate eggs. Beat whites until stiff, then gradually beat in 3/4 cup sugar. Beat yolks with remaining sugar until pale yellow and sugar is dissolved. Fold whites into yolk mixture. Fold in butter mixtures. Add flour mixture in 4 portions to make stiff dough.
With lightly floured hands, form into 4 cylinders, 1-1/2 inches in diameter and 8-10 inches long. Bake on lightly buttered cookie sheet for 30 minutes. Cool slightly, then cut into cookies 1/2" wide. Increase oven heat to 400, then bake, cut side down, for 5-10 minutes more, or until light brown. Makes about 80 cookies.

Robert James Waller

Robert Waller's first novel, The Bridges of Madison County, *became a phenomenon, one of the best selling books of all time, and is being made into a movie staring Clint Eastwood and Meryl Streep. His second novel,* Slow Dancing in Cedar Bend, *and a later collection of essays also became bestsellers. A photographer and musician as well as a writer, Waller is a professor at Iowa State University.*

I love chocolate and this is one of my favorite recipes.

Chocolate Chunk Brownies

1 cup butter or margarine
2 cups sugar
2 tsp. vanilla
4 eggs, slightly beaten
1 cup flour
1/2 cup unsweetened cocoa
1/2 tsp. salt
8 oz. (8 squares) semi-sweet chocolate, coarsely chopped

Heat oven to 350 degrees. Grease 13"x9" pan. In medium sauce pan over low heat, melt butter. Add sugar, vanilla and eggs. Blend well. Add flour, cocoa and salt. Blend well. Add chocolate chunks. Pour in prepared pan. Bake for 30 to 40 min. or until set. Cool. Cut into bars.
Note: I use the chunks that come in a bag from Hershey's. Saves a mess.

Luke Whisnant

Luke Whisnant's fiction has appeared in Esquire, Grand Street, Crescent Review, *and other publications. Two of his stories were reprinted in* New Stories From the South: The Year's Best *('86 and '87). He recently completed the screenplay based on his first novel,* Watching TV With the Red Chinese *and is working on a new novel,* Requiem for a Red Guitar. *He is associate professor of English at East Carolina University.*

This is a great side dish for summer cookouts or covered dish suppers, but I wouldn't serve it on a first date.

Second Date Greek Onion Salad

2 large sweet Vidalia onions, sliced
1/2 cup crumbled feta cheese
10 pitted black olives, sliced in half lengthways
1/2 tsp. sugar
A good quality Italian salad dressing
Lots of fresh-ground black pepper

Combine first 4 ingredients in a ceramic bowl. Add enough dressing to coat; grind plenty of pepper over the top. Mix well with a wooden spoon and add more pepper. Chill for an hour or so. Garnish with 1 more grind of pepper.

Jeanne Williams

One-time president of the Western Writers of America, Jeanne Williams won the Silver Spur Award for The Horsestalker *and* Freedom Trail. *She also has written historical and romance novels, as well as non-fiction and juvenile fiction. She lives in Portal, Arizona.*

I enjoy cooking and since I am vegetarian, serving my friends such foods is a bit of missionary work. I gave a tofu workshop at the Museum of Natural History's Southwest Research Station several years ago and the cook there still uses some of the recipes. Of course, in my books I never miss a chance to praise grains, fruits and vegetables and have had several vegetarian heroines.

In the mystery series that I hope to launch with the book I'm halfway through writing, the protagonist, Tory Field, runs a vegetarian bed & breakfast and restaurant, which, in cattle country like this, creates some humorous situations while allowing me to describe her tasty concoctions. If the series goes, a related cookbook would be a natural.

Now that studies prove that soy foods retard prostate cancer, it's more important than ever to work them into our diets. Tofu, for example, is a wonder food—no cholesterol, rich in protein and calcium and proved to retard that nemesis of virtually all older men, prostate cancer. It can be used in place of eggs in many recipes and adapts to everything from pudding to stroganoff. The key thing to remember is that it has no taste of its own but soaks up whatever it's mixed with, be it raspberries or garlic and onions.

Fruit Sherbert

2 parts frozen fruit—a mix of sliced bananas and berries is great—to 1 part soft tofu, 1 Tbsp. of lemon juice and sugar or honey to taste if the fruit isn't sweet enough. Whir in blender and serve. Frozen crushed pineapple is delicious in this. You get pudding by using unfrozen fresh or canned fruit. The potassium-rich bananas make this a terrific food for older folks.

Creamy Potato Soup

Saute 3 large sliced onions in canola oil. Add 6 or 7 sliced medium potatoes and simmer till done in just enough water to cover. Whip 12 or 16 oz. of soft tofu in blender or with hand beater and add along with 2 Tbsp. of dill, black pepper, 1/2 tsp. of salt and 3 Tbsp. of lemon juice. Stir well, heat thoroughly but don't boil. Let set for flavors to marry. Everyone will swear you used sour cream!

Quick Fiesta Corn Soup

Saute 1 large onion in canola oil. Chop up 1 or 2 red or green chilies, depending on how hot they are and how hot you like things. Saute with onion. Add 4 cups fresh, frozen or canned (no salt) corn and a cup of water or soy milk. Whip 12 or 16 oz. of soft tofu in blender and add. Stir till heated. 8 ounces of Soyco's Jalapeno Jack Cheese may be used in place of tofu and chilies for an even faster hearty meal.

Good health and happy feasting!

Index of Authors

Adams, Gail Galloway, 5
Auel, Jean, 10
Bache, Ellyn, 11
Barnes, Linda, 15
Barry, Dave, 17
Bishop, Michael, 19
Bledsoe, Jerry, 21
Blume, Judy, 23
Bond, Larry, 24
Bond, Michael, 26
Boyer, Rick, 28
Boyle, T. Coraghessan, 30
Bozzone, Bill, 32
Braun, Lilian Jackson, 33
Bridgers, Sue Ellen, 35
Brothers, Dr. Joyce, 36
Brown, Rosellen, 38
Budrys, Algis, 40
Card, Orson Scott, 41
Carlson, Ron, 43
Chappell, Fred, 45
Charnas, Suzy McKee, 47
Cherryh, C. J., 49
Clampitt, Amy, 51
Cline, Terry, 53
Cornwell, Bernard, 54
Cornwell, Patricia D., 59
Dailey, Janet, 61
D'Amato, Barbara, 62

De Lint, Charles, 64
Dillard, Annie, 66
Douglas, Carole Nelson, 68
Drake, David, 70
Edgerton, Clyde, 72
Flynt, Candace, 73
Foster, Alan Dean, 75
Gingher, Marianne, 77
Giovanni, Nikki, 79
Goode, James M., 81
Grafton, Sue, 82
Grant, Linda, 84
Halpern, Daniel, 86
Harrod-Eagles, Cynthia, 87
Hart, Carolyn, 89
Hecht, Anthony, 91
Hess, Joan, 93
Hillerman, Tony, 98
Hood, Ann, 100
Hurmence, Belinda, 102
Kellerman, Faye, 104
Kellerman, Jonathan, 106
King, Stephen, 107
Kline, Christina Baker, 109
Laker, Rosalind, 111
L'Engle, Madeleine, 112
MacLeod, Charlotte, 114
Maron, Margaret, 117
Matthews, Jack, 119
McCrumb, Sharyn, 120
McLaurin, Tim, 123
Michaels, Barbara, 125
Oleksiw, Susan, 126
Paretsky, Sara, 128
Pickard, Nancy, 130
Plain, Belva, 133
Raffel, Dawn, 134

Ragen, Naomi, 135
Redding, Sandra, 137
Richards, Judith, 139
Roberts, Les, 141
Sandlin, Tim, 142
Sandstrom, Eve, 144
Saul, John, 145
Shivers, Louise, 147
Siddons, Anne Rivers, 149
Spencer, Elizabeth, 151
Squire, Elizabeth Daniels, 153
Steele, Allen, 156
Tannen, Deboroh, 158
Taylor, Patricia, 161
Wallace, Marilyn, 164
Waller, Robert James, 166
Whisnant, Luke, 167
Williams, Jeanne, 168

Index of Recipes

Breads
    Charlotte's Tea Bread, 115
    Cora's Cornbread Delight, 46
    Cornbread from Mattie Rigsbee, 72
    Joe Robert's Fishing Cabin Cornbread, 45
    Pan Fried Cornbread, 124
Casseroles
    Baked Cheese Grits with Garlic, 124
    Eggplant Creole, 151
    Festive Green Bean Casserole, 93
    Hot Dog Casserole for Two, 74
    Jerusalem Kugel, 135
    Juanita Ortega's Chili Rellenos, 132
    Moussaka, 159
    Pig'n'Potato, 54
    Portuguese Sausage and Eggplant Casserole, 126
    Vegetable Casserole, 14
Chili Dishes
    Carlotta's Killer Chili, 15
    Eugenia Potter's 27-Ingredient Chili Con Carne, 130
    Kickapoo Chili, 142
    Libby Quarrels' Cowboy Carrot Chili, 19
Coffee Cakes
    Sweet Creativity Coffee Cake, 153
Desserts
    Apple Torte, 24
    Arly's Favorite Peach Cobbler, 96

    Capirotada (Mexican Bread Pudding), 132
    Cheesecake, 133
    Chilled Marble Cheesecake, 68
    Chocolate Chunk Brownies, 166
    Elizabeth MacPherson's Queen Elizabeth Cake, 120
    Fruit Sherbert, 169
    Golden Dream, 152
    Holiday Apricot Bars, 125
    Ice Box Cake, 134
    Mama Marilyn's Biscotti, 164
    Mary Lou's Chocolate Cake, 13
    My Mother's Bread Pudding, 81
    Norwegian Cream, 11
    Raspberry Brownies, 89
    Sweetheart Cherry Pie, 78
    The Walnut Wedding Cake, 147
Dressings
    Cupboard Fresh Dressing, 61
    Spinach Vinaigrette, 51
Egg Dishes
    Broccoli & Feta Omelet, 64
    Frittata Gabriella, 128
Fruit
    Gingered Fruit Glaze, 67
Meat
    Aromatic Beef from Java, 66
    Baked Camel (Stuffed), 30
    Chicken-Fried Steak With Cream Gravy, 94
    Frozen Lamb Shank in Clay Cooker, 79
    Judith's Tacos, 139
    "Katherine's" Beef Tenderloin, 73
    Meat Loaf, 36
    Navajo Tacos, 98
    Neck Bones and Noodles, 123
    Pig Pickin', 70
    Pork Liver Cupcakes (for Felines), 33
    Steak, 106

Toad in the Hole, 57
Miscellaneous
    Off-The-Wall Pizza, 156
    Updated Grandma's Sour Milk Rule, 154
Pancakes
    Coaster Pancakes, 40
    Zucchini-Feta Pancakes, 84
Pastas
    Lunchtime Gloop, 108
    Pasta Al Pesto, 62
    Ruote with Corn, Scallions and Coriander, 86
    Spaghetti Bolognese, 87
    Spaghetti Carbonara, 100
Poultry
    Chicken and Tarragon in a Creamy Tomato Sauce Over Linguine, 110
    Diced Chicken with Carrot/Mustard Suace and Rice, 49
    Jackanapes Fricassee, 119
    Maidie's Chicken Pastry, 117
    Milan Jacovich's "Chicken Village" Chicken Paprikash, 141
    Pollo Verde, 112
    Salsa Chicken, 104
Rice Dish
    Jacob's Guile, 47
Salads
    Artichoke Rice Salad, 35
    Estelle Oppers's Fancy Snowflake Salad, 95
    Rice-A-Roni Avocado Dinghies, 43
    Second Date Greek Onion Salad, 167
    Spinach Vinaigrette, 51
    Tomato and Pasta Salad, 162
Sandwiches
    Port Clyde Broccoli Salad Sandwich, 23
    The Kinsey Milhone Famous Peanut Butter & Pickle Sandwich, 82

Sauces
    Béchamel, 159
    Che Thomas's Guacamole, 132
    Lifetime Hot Sauce, 102
    Salsa Mexicana, 132
    Sauce Mornay, 27
    The One Necessary (Satay) Sauce, 38
Seafood
    Christmas Eve Scalloped Oysters, 149
    Crabby-Wabby Casserole, 145
    Doc's Baked Salmon with 3-C's Sauce, 28
    Floyd's Crab Cakes, 32
    Pan-Fried Garlic Piranha, 76
    Seafood Bledsonia, 22
    Shrimp and Okra Bisque, 6
Snacks or Hors d'Oeuvres
    O Calcutta Cheese Spread, 9
    Terry Cline's Lowest Cholesterol Roasted Pecans, 53
    Toast with Peanut Butter, 18
Soups
    Chef Dennis's Albondigas Soup, 131
    Creamy Potato Soup, 169
    Curried Butternut Squash Soup, 13
    Mild Gazpacho, 161
    Quick Fiesta Corn Soup, 169
    Stone Soup, 137
    Vegetable Beef Soup, 162
Stews
    American Feijoada, 41
    Gigi's Bean Pot Stew, 144
    Scarpetta's Stew, 59
Vegetables
    Baked Potatoes a la Pamplemousse, 26
    Beans 'n Ham, 95
    Byzantine Artichokes, 92
    Curried Green Tomatoes, 161
    Potatoes and Carrots, 10